Rolled, Wrapped, and Stuffed

Other Books by Janet Hazen

Glories of the Vegetarian Table

The Sophisticated Sandwich

New Game Cuisine

Rolled Wrapped and Stuffed

Great Appetizers from Around the World

BY JANET HAZEN

PHOTOGRAPHY BY
JOYCE OUDKERK POOL

Aris Books

Addison-Wesley Publishing Company, Inc.
Reading, Massachusetts   Menlo Park, California
New York   Don Mills, Ontario   Wokingham, England
Amsterdam   Bonn   Sydney   Singapore   Tokyo
Madrid   San Juan   Paris   Seoul   Milan
Mexico City   Taipei

Library of Congress Cataloging-in-Publication Data

Hazen, Janet.
    Rolled, wrapped, and stuffed: great appetizers from around the
world / Janet Hazen.
        p. cm.
    Includes index.
    ISBN 0-201-57077-7
    1. Appetizers.   2. Cookery, International.   I. Title.
TX740.H33   1991
641.8'12—dc20   90-19604
                                                          CIP

Cover and text design by Ingalls + Associates
Designer: Tracy Dean
Food Stylist: Sue White

Set in 12-point Garamond #3 by
NK Graphics, Keene, NH.
Separations by Color Associates, Inc.,
St. Louis, MO.
Printed and bound by Arcata Kingsport,
Kingsport, TN, on 70-pound Warrenflo stock
from Lindenmeyr Paper Company.

1 2 3 4 5 6 7 8 9-KP-9594939291
First printing, February 1991

Acknowledgments

I would like to thank Joyce Oudkerk Pool, Dawn Collins, and Sue White for their ultimate good taste, patience, and team work . . . as well as all the back rubs, cocktails, coffee, constant attention, furious laughter, and combined winning personalities.

Thank you, Tom Ingalls, for your singular sense of design and joyous humor.

Thanks to Tracy Dean and Kendra Lawrence.

I would like to thank Michael Miller and Edward Brown at Accession; Stephanie Thompson at Poveri Fiori; Alta Tingle at The Gardner; Stephanie Greenleigh; Sandra Griswold; Sue Fisher King; Artifacts, San Francisco; and Daniel Bowe for props. Thanks to Missy Hamilton for her outstanding backgrounds and plates.

Thank you, John Harris, for giving me color photographs, oohing and aahing over my food, and working so closely with me on my favorite book.

Thank you, Greg Kaplan, for your attention and work on the manuscript, and especially for smoothing the furrowed brow.

Thanks to Claudia Oudkerk Pool for help in the kitchen and on the set.

TABLE OF CONTENTS

Chicken-and-
Vegetable Mosaic

Ham-and-Water-
Chestnut Fried Wontons
with Corn Relish

Roast Duck-Lettuce
Packages with Apricot-
Ginger Chutney

LIST OF RECIPES

Basics

Asian

Italian

Middle Eastern and Russian

Mediterranean

Latin American and Caribbean

Cross Cultural

INTRODUCTION

I think it all started with Oreo cookies. It wasn't the funny-textured chocolate cookie, and it wasn't the stark white, sugary filling—it was the combination of the two. Although I was accused of playing with my food, I remember I had several distinct ways of eating Oreos. The concept of a *filled* sweet was delightful to me. I moved on to éclairs, and finally graduated to savory but simple foods such as manicotti, calzone, and wontons. I was fascinated with things that had creamy or spicy insides, like delicate doughs wrapped around surprise fillings and jewel-like goodies rolled up in crisp lettuce leaves. These humble dishes were my introduction to rolled, wrapped, and stuffed foods, and, over the years, I have sought out, both in my professional capacity as a chef and a food writer as well as a passionate eater, these delicacies in every shape and form.

I also love appetizers made of pastes spread on crackers or bread; dips that beg for chips, vegetables, or bread sticks; and little skewers of grilled meats, fish, and poultry. Although there are thousands of wonderful appetizers that don't fit into the rolled, wrapped, and stuffed category, my preference is for the mysterious and complex. A wrapped appetizer can be as simple as a spinach leaf wrapped around several savory ingredients, as in Thai Spinach Packages (page 31), or as elaborate as Trinidadian Pork Pastelles (page 104). Many vegetables can be stuffed, and a myriad of doughs, wrappers, and sliced or flattened meats, poultry, and fish can be filled and rolled into tubes. The choices are almost endless, and this kind of food makes some of the most rewarding I've ever tasted.

Traditionally, appetizers are small appetite teasers served before a large meal, and are usually accompanied with drinks of some sort. Called *tapas* in Spain, *antojitos* in Latin countries, *hors d'oeuvre* in France, *mezze* in the Middle East, *antipasti* in Italy, *zakuski* in Russia, "street food" or "snacks" in Asia and the Caribbean, and simply *appetizers* in the United States, these little pleasures can range from a simple bowl of olives to an elaborate concoction of several complex dishes. All cuisines have appetizers, and the range of ingredients, flavors, textures, and styles of preparation is staggering.

The current trend in eating lighter food is here to stay. The popular *tapas* bars of Spain, where lively groups of people stand at bars sipping sherry or wine and sampling a vast assortment of small dishes, have greatly influenced eating styles in restaurants and bars throughout the United States. This form of snacking plays an important role in the way we perceive dining, whether in a formal restaurant, a casual cafe, or in our homes. At last, Americans have realized that several smaller plates of food can be more interesting than one large plate filled to the brim with meat, fish, or poultry, a vegetable, and a starch.

Restaurant-goers know that often the best food on the menu is found in the list of appetizers. Here we commonly see condensed flavors, interesting presentations, alluring designs, and creative combinations of food. Chefs often feel that they can experiment more with an appetizer than with an entree, thus creating an exciting invention of flavors, textures, and colors. As a result, diners find themselves choosing several appetizers rather than one main dish.

Most people like to have a choice when it comes to food. The beauty of appetizers is that they are so flexible; the quintessential entertainment food, they don't have to be saved just for pre-dinner occasions. A cocktail party wouldn't be a cocktail party without an assortment of hors d'oeuvres. Many appetizers can be served for brunch, lunch, a light supper, as a snack, or combined to make a full meal. Since many of the snack foods of Asia, Mexico, and the Caribbean are prepared in the morning to be kept at room temperature all day, they are suitable for bringing along on a picnic, or in the car when traveling. Many of the recipes in this collection are perfect to bring to a friend's house for an event. Many of the recipes also can be prepared in large quantities, frozen, and served for spontaneous social gatherings, while others are so simple and quick to make, you can dash to the kitchen to prepre a dazzling appetizer or two while your guests enjoy a glass of wine. The way you choose to serve these dishes is up to you—the sky is the limit.

A large number of the following recipes were inspired by my travels. Having visited Thailand, Malaysia, Singapore, Mexico, Portugal, Canada, and the Caribbean, I feel a strong connection with many of the dishes from these countries. Living in San Francisco, with its diverse population and its many wonderful restaurants, has also given me the opportunity to sample well-prepared, authentic, and delicious dishes from around the world. While I treasure my memories of eating delightful foods in their country of origin, the second-best thing to being there is re-creating the flavors and dishes that make those memories special.

This book is divided into ethnic chapters. Certain countries are more famous for their rolled, wrapped, or stuffed dishes than others. Mexican and Asian cuisines are particularly noted for this style of food. When I compiled a list of dishes to include in this book, I realized that some of the preparations couldn't really be confined to one category. Is a Mexican flauta rolled or stuffed? These categories are a simple way to define different kinds of appetizers, but the book is based on the firm belief that rolled, wrapped, and stuffed foods are delicious, fun to eat, and a perfect way to entertain.

While some traditional regional dishes are flawless, others need a little improvement. Some of the more traditional Middle Eastern and Russian dishes are too one-dimensional, and while they were perfectly acceptable at the time of their creation, they now call for some updating by means of additional spices, herbs, meats, or vegetables. Many of the recipes in each ethnic category are fairly classic, but a few have had some minor adjustments. For example, Chinese pork buns traditionally are made with an unyeasted dough using baking powder as the leavening agent. Although I tried a baking powder dough, it simply didn't work. Yeasted dough makes fluffy, tender, and very light pork buns, and many of the buns I have sampled in dim sum houses in New York, California, Washington, and Canada were made with yeast. The Fried Ham-and-Fontina Tortillas with Red Pepper–Ancho Sauce (page 108) is not a classic Mexican dish, but the techniques and some of the ingredients are true to Latin American cooking. Some of the recipes developed for this book draw on regional ingredients and cooking styles, but result in original and unique appetizers, and these are included in the section of cross-cultural recipes.

It is important to read the Basics section before starting to cook from this book. While there aren't any difficult or tricky steps involved in these recipes, it is best to familiarize yourself with the different techniques used in preparing some of the more unusual or ethnic dishes. Most ingredients are easy to come by these days, and if you don't have access to exotic produce, dried goods, or spices from a local ethnic market, chances are a nearby major grocery store will carry many of these items.

Quite a few of these recipes involve making a dough for a wrapper. The Asian and Latino recipes usually use pre-made wrappers such as wonton wrappers, pot sticker and egg roll skins, rice papers, banana leaves, or flour or corn tortillas. Since almost every cuisine has a form of savory pie such as *samosas*, dumplings, empanadas, and calzones, learning how to make dough is essential. Such two-step preparations are a bit time-consuming, so allow plenty of time, and get a helper or two if you plan to make a large recipe of this sort for a party. The beauty of many of these particular recipes is that the two steps, the filling and the dough, can be prepared over a period of two days. Nine times out of ten, the filling improves with age and will taste better the second day. Making fillings one day before you want to assemble the dish not only allows the ingredients of the filling to "marry," but also gives you plenty of time to prepare the dough. Certain doughs can even be prepared one day, refrigerated, and rolled out the next. I often make a dough, roll it out into the desired shape, individually wrap each piece of dough in sheets of plastic wrap, and refrigerate them until I am ready to fill, wrap, and assemble the next day. These filled dough recipes are thus very flexible, and are for the most part easy to prepare.

Culinary America is coming into its own, and while many of us have been enjoying ethnic foods for years, others are just discovering exotic cuisines for the first time. Contemporary American cuisine can best be described as a mirror of our wonderfully diverse culture. Every country of the world has classic dishes that truly represent its indigenous ingredients, cultural habits, and age-old culinary traditions. Contemporary American cooking takes these classics and presents them in new, sometimes playful ways, or modifies them to suit personal tastes. This exchange creates an ever changing global cuisine that essentially is a form of sharing among individuals, regions, and countries. In this book you will find both a personal approach to some of the world's favorite appetizers, and a cross-cultural style of cooking that draws inspiration from friends, families, towns, cities, states, and countries.

I

Basics: Techniques, Recipes, and Serving Suggestions

I

Basics: Techniques,
Recipes, and Serving
Suggestions

The recipes in this book are fairly straightforward, and executing them does not require any unusual or professional cooking skills. There are, however, a few basic techniques that could help you, not only when preparing dishes from this book, but in your everyday cooking.

I suggest looking this chapter over before you begin cooking from this book, so that you will be more familiar with certain procedures. This is not a complete chapter on general cooking techniques, but it covers most of the basic steps used to make these dishes.

While some of the sauces and doughs may seem similar to one another, they are all different, and are suited for each particular recipe. Two recipes that are used more than once in the book are included in this chapter: Basic Bread Dough (page 12), and Basic Chicken Stock (page 13).

SERVING SUGGESTIONS

Most of the dishes in this book can be served on large platters or on smaller, individual plates. Some of the more complex sauced dishes require plates, forks, and knives, and are best served at the table, before the meal. When a recipe has a "dipping sauce," the sauce can be served in a small bowl placed near the platter of food, or directly on the platter, if space permits. Each dish and its accompanying sauce make a complete flavor package, with ingredients, textures, and colors combining to complement one another. This doesn't mean, however, that your guests will observe these boundaries. When I give parties, I like to place the appropriate bowl of sauce as close to the food as possible, but invariably people will start to experiment with foods and different sauces, and pretty soon everyone is dipping his or her tidbits of food into every sauce on the table. This is just fine, and in fact, it can create exciting flavor combinations and give your guests an opportunity to try new ingredients and flavors. Very few of the dishes in this book have sauces that go directly on or underneath the finished dish. However, when this is the case, the recipe will specify where and how the sauce should be served. Generally speaking, fried foods are never served in a sauce, as they will become soggy and limp, and their texture will be ruined. Therefore, dipping sauces are perfect for most fried foods.

A Note on Portions

It is impossible to give an exact figure for how many appetizers each dinner guest will consume. There are countless variables that need to be taken into account when deciding the quantity of food to be prepared. Generally, it is safe to say that the average dinner guest will want three to four individual appetizers before a meal. That figure will increase to approximately eight to ten if the meal is to be made up of appetizers. Each recipe in the book gives a yield, such as 24 pieces, packages, slices, or so on. With that information, you can figure out how many dishes will be needed to serve your party. A suggestion: if you're planning on making an entire meal of appetizers, I would highly recommend serving them with a light green salad.

TECHNIQUES

Cooking Chicken Breasts

When a recipe calls for cooked chicken meat, buy one or two whole chicken breasts, or a whole cut-up chicken if you would like to use both dark and white meat. Cook the chicken by placing the breasts or whole chicken in a large pot with cold water to cover. Bring to a boil, reduce the heat to moderate, and cook, uncovered, for 20 to 25 minutes, for breasts, depending on size. To check for doneness, remove one of the breasts and pierce the thickest part of the breast with a sharp knife. If the juice runs clear and the meat is opaque all the way to the bone, the meat is done. Do not overcook the chicken or it will be dry, tough, and tasteless. Remove the chicken from the water and cool in a colander or on a rack. When cool enough to handle, remove the meat from the bones, taking care to separate and discard the cartilage and skin.

Save the cooking liquid, bones, and scraps for making stock. If you add the bones, some uncooked chicken pieces, a couple of carrots, 2 onions, some parsley, and 2 quarts of water, you can made a fine pot of chicken stock; see Basic Chicken Stock (page 13).

Cooking Dry Beans

It is difficult to ruin a pot of beans, but there are a few important guidelines to follow when cooking legumes.

Soaking beans shortens the cooking time, and it also allows some of the gas-producing enzymes to be released before cooking. Try to soak beans for at least 8 hours before cooking, or preferably for 24 hours, changing the water every 6 to 8 hours.

Do not salt beans while they cook, because this toughens them. They do, however, require quite a bit of salt to bring out their flavor, so if you are not on a sodium-restricted diet, salt the finished product liberally. Acids, such as vinegar and wine, also can toughen beans and prevent them from softening.

Usually beans are cooked in stock or broth with spices, herbs, onions, garlic, and sometimes tomatoes or chilies. But if you want the unadulterated bean without other flavors, cook the beans in plain water. If you are not using the cooked beans right away, you may store them, covered, in their cooled cooking liquid or drained, in the refrigerator for up to 5 days. Cooked beans may be frozen for up to 2 to 3 months.

Cooking Onions

Many of the recipes in this book call for onions and garlic cooked in oil. When a recipe reads, "Cook the onions in oil over moderate heat for 10 minutes," but does not specify the color or texture of the onions, then the 10 minutes of cooking is all that is required for that particular dish. When it is important to cook the onions until they are golden brown, deep brown, not brown at all, or translucent, the recipe will give this direction.

Cooking with Hot Chilies

Several varieties of hot chilies are used throughout this book. Most commonly called for are jalapeño chilies, which are found in most grocery, Latino, and Asian food stores. Avoid touching sensitive areas of your body after you have worked with hot chilies, and if you are particularly sensitive, you may want to wear rubber gloves while cutting chilies.

Always remove the stem of any chili before adding the chili to the other ingredients. The seeds and ribs contain the most capsaicin, which gives the chili its characteristic "heat." Seeds add body, flavor, texture, and heat, and sometimes should be left in the finished dish. When this is not desired, the recipe will call for chilies to be seeded first, and if it isn't important to remove the seeds and ribs, the recipe will simply call for the pepper to be minced, chopped, or sliced.

Cooking Rice

I like to use a method called free boiling to cook rice. This is a technique similar to cooking pasta. To cook 1 to 2 cups of any kind of rice, bring 6 cups of water to a boil in a large, heavy-bottomed saucepan. When the water is boiling, add the rice and stir with a fork until the water returns to a boil. Cook over high heat until the rice is tender. Drain in a fine colander and let cool before using. Rice can be cooked and stored in a covered container in the refrigerator for up to 5 days.

Deep-Fat Frying

Deep-frying is not very popular these days, but there are certain dishes that not only benefit from this type of cooking, but are successful only when cooked in this manner.

The ultimate goal when deep-fat frying is to produce food that is cooked all the way through, is crispy, and is as grease-free as possible. All this can be achieved with relative ease if you follow a few simple steps.

Oils labeled "vegetable oil" are the best to use when frying food. Vegetable oil—usually a combination of various oils—is virtually tasteless and has a very high smoking point, meaning that it can be heated to high temperatures without smoking or burning. Cottonseed, corn, safflower, and peanut oils are also used for deep-fat frying. Lard, which has a very distinctive flavor, and Crisco are both solid at room temperature, and are favored in the deep South in the United States and in parts of Europe. I recommend using vegetable oil for most of the recipes in this book.

A large, heavy, deep pot should be used for all deep-fat frying. As the oil heats, it expands, and when food is added, it often bubbles fiercely and rises in the pot. For this reason alone, a large pot, big enough to accommodate the expansion of the oil and the food, should be used. Fill the vessel only one-half full of oil. Have handy a slotted spoon or a shallow sieve to remove the food when it is done. Most food should be drained on paper towels, so be sure to have these laid out ahead of time on a flat surface.

The second most important factor is the temperature of the oil. If you are using a regulated deep-fat fryer, you will not have to gauge the temperature of the oil yourself, but if you are using a regular saucepan, then you must carefully watch the temperature of the oil. If the oil is too hot, it will not cook the food thoroughly, and if it is not hot enough, the food will be soggy, limp, and greasy. The approximate temperature for deep-fat frying is 350° to 375° F. If you do not have a deep-fat thermometer, you can test the oil by dropping a cube of bread into the hot fat. If the bread browns in about 1 minute, the oil is right for cooking, around 365° F. If the fat begins to smoke, reduce the heat and continue cooking. However, if the oil smokes for more than a couple of minutes, chances are the oil is burned and will impart a bitter and unpleasant taste to anything cooked in it. Discard such oil and start over with clean, new oil. When you consider the cost of oil compared to the amount of time and energy you put into making the food, discarding burned oil is more sensible than ruining a whole batch of good food.

When you are finished with the hot oil, leave it on the stove to cool to room temperature. When it is cool, you may strain it through a fine wire mesh to remove any food particles if you plan to use it again. If the oil is very dark and you have cooked quite a bit of food in it, you may want to discard it.

In most cases, food to be fried should be cold. This helps it to stay intact while cooking. It also helps to make the exterior golden brown, and prevents excess oil from seeping into the interior. Food should always be dry, whether it is coated with flour, bread crumbs, or finely chopped nuts. Excessive moisture will interrupt the natural frying process and can make for limp, soggy foods.

Preparing Ginger

Try to use fresh ginger instead of powdered ginger. The fresh root has a hot, spicy, pungent flavor and aroma, and it adds flavor and complexity to foods. Choose firm, unblemished roots, with relatively smooth, light brown skin and a hard texture.

Always peel the root, using a paring knife, removing the thin, outer skin. Some people like to grate the ginger, which produces a finer product, but leaves the "hairs," or fibers, of the root mixed in with the flesh. This can affect the texture of the food, and is unpleasant in some cases. For this reason, I always like to mince ginger, rather than grating it finely. To mince peeled ginger, simply slice it into very thin pieces lengthwise, then, using a very sharp knife, mince it into tiny pieces. Fresh ginger can be stored at room temperature in a dark, cool, dry place for up to 2 months.

Roasting Peppers

Any type of fresh pepper or chili can be cooked over a gas flame, over coals, or even in a very hot oven, but the best methods are over flames or coals. The intense heat of the flame or coals chars the thin layer of skin on the pepper, turning it black and infusing the flesh with a desirable smoky flavor. The skin is then peeled away and the seeds are removed, leaving a silky, slightly cooked pepper. If the pepper is cooked too long, the flesh too will begin to char and disintegrate, and very little edible flesh will remain.

To roast peppers over a gas flame or over coals: Using tongs or a very long fork, hold the pepper over the hottest part of the flame, rotating it until all the sides *just* turn black. Place the pepper in a plastic or paper bag and let it "steam," or "sweat," for about 20 minutes or up to several hours. When the pepper is cool enough to handle, gently remove the black skin, stem, and seeds. It may be helpful to peel the charred skin under cold running water. The pepper is now ready for eating or using in recipes.

To roast in an oven: Place the peppers on a baking sheet in an oven preheated to 450° F. Bake for 20 to 25 minutes, or until the peppers are very soft and light brown, and the skin has become thin and puffy and separates from the flesh. The skin will not be blackened, as it is when roasting over flames or charcoal, but it will be seared enough to remove it, leaving a lightly cooked pepper with a mild smoky flavor.

Slicing Soft Cheese

Slicing soft cheeses like mozzarella, Monterey Jack, or Bel Paese can seem impossible at times, but if you use a serrated knife the job can be accomplished without frustration. Refrigerate the cheese for at least 2 hours before slicing. Remove it from the refrigerator and place it on a flat surface. Using a sharp serrated knife, slice the cheese, using a sawing motion, into the desired thickness.

Steaming Foods

Steaming is a moist-heat method of cooking food. The boiling water does not come in contact with the food, but rather the steam it produces, combined with the heat of the pot and lid, cooks the product indirectly. When you steam food, the pot must always be covered, and the water should never touch the food.

The best way to steam is to use a large bamboo steamer set in a large wok filled with boiling water, or an electric steamer. I prefer Chinese bamboo steamers because they are big enough to hold a large portion of the total yield of most recipes, and they can be stacked, making a two-tier steaming unit. You can buy these round steamers at Asian markets and gourmet cookware stores. Electric steamers are smaller but work just as well. If you do not have a steamer, you can make one by placing a large, heatproof metal rack or a collapsible metal steamer in the bottom of a very large pot. Add water to the pan, making sure it doesn't touch the rack. Bring the water to boil, place the food on the rack, cover the pot with a tight-fitting lid, and cook until the food is done.

Toasting Nuts and Seeds

Toasting nuts and seeds heightens their flavor and makes them crunchy. Place the nuts or seeds on a baking sheet and spread them evenly, making a single layer. Bake in a preheated 350° F oven for 5 to 12 minutes, depending on the types of nuts. Large dense nuts such as filberts, cashews, hazelnuts, and almonds require more time. Pine nuts, walnuts, pecans, peanuts, sesame seeds, and pumpkin seeds are more fragile and don't take as long to toast. Toast nuts or seeds in the oven until they are golden brown and their fragrance fills the air. Remove from the pan and cool on a flat surface. Some nuts are soggy when they first come out of the oven, but as they cool they become crisp and crunchy.

A faster, but less thorough way to toast nuts or seeds is to use a sauté pan. Place the nuts in a dry sauté pan or skillet and cook over moderate heat, shaking the pan or stirring frequently, until the nuts or seeds are golden brown. Remove from pan and cool on a flat surface.

Working with Various Doughs, Wrappers, and Papers

Many types of doughs, wrappers, and papers are used in this book, and each has different and unique characteristics. Filo, pie, bread, and Chinese pork-bun dough, rice paper, egg roll and pot sticker skins, wonton wrappers, and tortilla dough are used in these recipes. All the doughs and store-bought skins and wrappers are easy to use and do not require any special training or equipment. There are a few basic steps to follow when making or using each dough, and once you are familiar with the qualities of each product, you will find that they are very easy to use.

Yeasted Doughs

Recipes using yeasted doughs in this book are Chinese Steamed Pork Buns (page 42), Three-Meat-and-Cheese Bread Roll (page 58), Sausage-and-Cheese Mini Calzones (page 60), Herb-and-Garlic Bread Sticks (page 64), and Fish-and-Rice Rastegai (page 81).

Leavening agents: All of the yeasted doughs in this book use active dry yeast as the leavening agent. It is sold in a three-strip, dated package in the baking section of the grocery store. Each package contains about ¼ ounce, or 2 teaspoons. The yeast must be dissolved in warm water (105° to 115° F) in order for it to become activated. Higher temperatures will kill the yeast, and lower temperatures will not activate the yeast.

Kneading the dough: To knead dough, first turn it out onto a lightly floured surface. With the heel of your hand, push the dough away from you, starting from the center of the dough mass. Gently bring the far edge of the dough over the top surface and down to the bottom of the dough mass, folding it over on itself. Give the dough a quarter turn and repeat the procedure. Knead the dough in this fashion for 3 to 10 minutes, or until the dough is smooth and elastic.

Proofing dough: Place the dough in a lightly greased bowl and cover it with a damp towel or plastic wrap. Let sit in a warm place (about 80° F) such as a gas oven with a pilot light, for 1 to 4 hours, or until doubled in size. To test the dough, poke your finger into the dough ball; if the indentation remains, the dough has risen enough. The recipes in this book do not require a second rising, so the dough is ready to be portioned out at this point.

Portioning the dough: When a recipe calls for 12 dough balls, it is easiest to divide the dough into larger balls first, making the smaller portions from the larger balls. For example, divide the dough into 2 equal balls. To make 12 equal-sized balls, divide the 2 dough balls into 2 equal balls. At this point you should have 4 equal-sized balls. Divide each ball into 3 equal-sized balls, leaving 12 dough balls. Using this method makes it easy to gauge the size of each portion, ensuring an evenly cooked and evenly browned product.

Letting the dough rest: After the dough is portioned, it must rest at room temperature or it will be too springy and difficult to work with. Cover the portioned dough with a damp towel or plastic wrap, and allow it to sit at room temperature for 30 minutes to 1 hour, or until the dough does not spring back when it is poked with a finger.

Rolling and forming dough: Most dough requires a little flour on the rolling surface, which prevents the dough from sticking to the table, the rolling pin, and your hands. Gently flatten a dough ball into a disc shape. Place on a lightly floured surface. Using a rolling pin, roll the dough into an even, flat, circular shape. Be sure to roll in each direction several times, as this makes the circle more uniform in shape and size.

Storing rolled-out dough: Usually there is enough flour on the dough rounds to prevent them from sticking to each other, but to be safe, it is a good idea to layer the circles between waxed paper, parchment paper, or plastic wrap. Certain doughs will stick to aluminum foil, so avoid using foil when stacking and wrapping rolled-out dough circles.

Sealing dough: It isn't always necessary to use a special sealing compound such as egg, butter, or cornstarch with yeasted dough, but a few recipes call for egg sealer or wash. This helps the dough stick to itself, making a tight seal, and prevents the filling from leaking while baking.

Unyeasted Doughs

Recipes using unyeasted dough in this book are Curried Malaysian Packets (page 40), Jamaican Beef Patties (page 105), Kasha Knishes (page 97), and Meat-and-Mushroom Piroshki (page 80).

There are a few dough recipes that are made with all-purpose flour, butter or oil, salt, and just a little water to bring it together. These doughs are generally richer than the yeasted variety, and have a more crumbly, tender, buttery texture.

Very little kneading, if any, is required with this type of dough. At most, 2 to 3 minutes of kneading is sufficient to bring the ingredients together and make the dough uniform and smooth. Overkneading unyeasted doughs can make them tough and dry. While unyeasted dough does not have to rise, it does benefit from resting at room temperature for at least 1 hour before it is portioned into small balls.

Filo Dough

Recipes using filo dough in this book are Vegetable-Olive–filled Filo Rolls (page 86), Mediterranean Filo Rounds (page 87), Briouates with Assorted Fillings (page 96), and Spanakopita (page 90).

Filo dough is a special Middle Eastern dough made from flour, salt, and water. The dough is made in very large paper-thin sheets, and is sprinkled with cornstarch to prevent the sheets from sticking together. Filo dough is sold in 1-pound boxes, and is usually found in the frozen-foods section of grocery stores, specialty markets, or ethnic food stores. It can be kept frozen for several months, or refrigerated for about 1 week. It must be kept in a plastic bag or it will dry out and become unusable.

Filo dough is easy to work with, despite its delicate nature. The dough is traditionally brushed with melted unsalted butter, and finely chopped nuts, bread crumbs, or a combination of both are sprinkled between each sheet. This process gives the finished product its characteristically flaky texture, rich flavor, and golden brown color. Some people like to use margarine, or even olive oil, but neither gives the dough the richness, taste, or color that butter does.

When using filo dough, always cover the big stack with a damp towel or plastic wrap. The sheets dry out very quickly and are unusable in this condition. Make sure the butter is completely melted before brushing it onto a sheet of dough. A minimal amount of butter should be used on each sheet, with only about 1½ tablespoons of crumbs or finely chopped nuts per layer. The final layer, or the top of each packet, should always be brushed with melted butter before baking. It is easier to slice a filo dough dish if you let it sit for 10 minutes after removing it from the oven.

Rice Paper Rounds

Recipes using rice paper rounds in this book are Vietnamese Rice Noodle Rolls with Peanut Sauce (page 34) and Vietnamese Imperial Rolls with Nuoc Mam Sauce (page 35).

Rice paper rounds are made from rice flour, salt, and water. The thin, translucent dough is then dried on bamboo mats, which gives the papers their characteristic cross-hatch pattern. They come in 6-, 8-, or 13-inch rounds, and can be stored wrapped in a plastic bag at room temperature for several months.

When using rice papers, be sure to cover the large stack with a damp towel or plastic wrap to prevent the papers from drying out, curling up, and absorbing moisture. They will be impossible to use in this condition. To make the papers pliable, fill a very large bowl with cold water. Dip a sheet of rice paper into the water for 2 seconds, remove, and lay flat on a dry surface. The dough will become pliable within seconds. It can be filled and rolled at this point, and served raw as in Vietnamese Rice Noodle Rolls, or fried as in Vietnamese Imperial Rolls.

Eggroll, Wonton, or Pot Sticker Wrappers and Skins

Recipes using wrappers or skins in this book are Chinese Egg Rolls with Mustard Dipping Sauce (page 38), Chinese Pot Stickers (page 44), Burmese Samosas with Hot Chili Dipping Sauce (page 26), and Ham-and-Water Chestnut Fried Wontons (page 126).

Wrappers are made from flour, eggs, oil, and salt, and are sprinkled with cornstarch to prevent one layer from sticking to another. They can be purchased in grocery stores, Asian markets, and specialty-food stores, and are usually found in the produce department or the frozen foods section. Wrappers vary in size, shape, and thickness. Egg roll wrappers are large rectangles, wonton wrappers are small squares, and pot sticker skins are thinner than the others, and round. This dough is very easy to work with, and does not dry out as quickly as rice papers or filo dough, but covering the large stack of dough with a damp towel or plastic wrap is still a good idea. A slurry made from 3 tablespoons of cornstarch dissolved in about 1 cup of cold water is an excellent compound to seal the edges of these doughs. Wrapped foods can be steamed, fried, baked, deep-fried, or boiled. They are very versatile and quite inexpensive.

Tortilla Dough

Recipes using tortilla dough in this book are Gorditas (page 110), Trinidadian Pork Pastelles (page 104), and Papusas (page 116).

Tortilla dough is made from ground dried yellow, white, or blue corn; lime; salt; and just enough water to make the dough pliable and soft. *Masa harina,* a commercial product, contains all of these ingredients and, mixed with water, makes a fine tortilla dough. *Masa harina* can be purchased in Latino grocery stores and most major supermarkets.

This dough does not have a leavening agent, and requires only enough kneading to combine the ingredients. It can be made and used immediately, but benefits from a short resting period before rolling. The dough can be wrapped in plastic and stored in the refrigerator for 2 to 3 days.

Basic Bread Dough

This dough is not used to make loaves, but for calzones, bread rolls, etc.

1 cup unbleached bread flour
1 cup unbleached all-purpose flour
1 teaspoon salt
⅔ cup warm water (105° to 115° F)

1 package (2½ teaspoons) active dry yeast
3 tablespoons olive oil

*P*lace the flours and salt in a large bowl and mix well. Place the warm water in a small bowl and add the yeast. Mix to dissolve the yeast and add the olive oil. Slowly add the yeast mixture to the flour, mixing with your hand or a wooden spoon as you go. When all the liquid has been added, mix the dough, forming it into a ball. If the dough is too wet, add flour by 1 tablespoon increments, but only enough to make it workable. If the dough is too dry, add a little more water.

Turn the dough out onto a lightly floured surface and knead for 3 to 4 minutes, or until the dough is pliable and smooth. Place in a lightly greased bowl, turn to coat the dough, and cover with a damp towel or plastic wrap. Place in a warm place (about 80° F) to rise. An oven with a pilot light is perfect. Let the dough rise until doubled in size, about 2 to 2½ hours, depending on the temperature of the room or oven.

Remove the dough from the bowl and punch down. (If you were making bread, you would let the dough rise one more time, but the recipes in this book require only one rising.)

Turn the dough out onto a lightly floured surface and knead for 3 minutes.

Cover the dough with a damp towel and allow to rest at room temperature for 20 minutes, or until it no longer turns back on itself when rolled.

At this point the dough is ready to be rolled into bread sticks, pizza, calzone, bread rolls, or savory pie shapes.

Basic Chicken Stock

Makes about 8 cups

4 pounds mixed chicken backs and
  wings
4 quarts cold water

2 large onions, coarsely chopped
4 carrots, peeled and coarsely
  chopped
4 celery stalks, coarsely chopped
2 bay leaves

*P*lace the chicken pieces in a large stockpot and cover with cold water. Bring to a boil over high heat and skim the surface of foam. Add the remaining ingredients and bring to a second boil. Reduce the heat to moderate and simmer for 3 to 4 hours, adding more water as it cooks away. Cool slightly, strain through a collander, and store, covered, in the refrigerator for up to 5 days, or freeze for up to 2 months.

II

Menus

II

Menus

If you are planning a party, choose an assortment of appetizers that complement one another. Depending on the time of year, whether your party is formal or casual, and the culinary theme, if any, choose four to six different dishes that showcase seasonal produce (see "Note on Portions" page 3). It is nice to have several hot dishes along with some room-temperature dishes. Consider the colors, textures, flavors, and serving style of each recipe, and how they combine with other dishes. Be sure to choose a few that can be made ahead and stored in the refrigerator before serving. Garnish your plates and the tables imaginatively: fresh herbs, edible flowers, ribbons, and compatible linens and tableware can make a stunning presentation. If you are choosing recipes from only one ethnic group, you might want to serve the food on plates and platters that reflect the style of that particular culture. Try to plan a decorating theme for your party if you want to serve all Asian, all Latin American, or all Russian appetizers. This will make for a memorable occasion, and will be fun for you as well. Conversely, a cross-cultural cocktail party or dinner will most likely thrill your guests.

It is nice to serve compatible beverages with a theme party. While wine seems to be the beverage of choice these days, and certainly goes well with most everything, it is also fun to serve iced vodka with Russian *zakuski;* tequila and limes with *antojitos;* Thai or Chinese beer with Asian food; exotic rum and tropical mixed drinks with Caribbean fare; ouzo with Greek or Middle Eastern *mezze;* and sherry or aperitifs with Mediterranean hors d'oeuvres. There are no rules when it comes to serving food—you can mix and match—but make sure you have a good selection of light dishes mixed with substantial ones, and a pleasing assortment of flavors, ingredients, colors, and textures. The most important thing to remember when giving a party is to relax, enjoy your guests, and have as much of the food prepared and ready to serve when your guests arrive as possible. If you are exhausted from cooking all day, you won't be able to have fun at your own party.

Following are some menu suggestions for parties large and small. Certainly you are free to pick and choose your own selection of appetizers from the book, but if you aren't sure which dishes would go best together, you can choose one or two of the following menus. There are straightforward ethnic menus, as well as cross-cultural menus that combine several compatible dishes from various countries or regions.

A Mixed Asian Menu

Here is a selection of both light and substantial dishes, vegetable and starch dishes, and hot and cold.

Tuna Tartare–stuffed Cucumbers (page 27)

Thai Spicy Pork-and-Vegetable–stuffed Squid (page 30)

Thai Spinach Packages with Five Jewels and Chili-Honey Sauce
(page 31)

Curried Malaysian Packets with Peanut Dipping Sauce (page 40)

Chinese Steamed Pork Buns (page 42)

A Southeast Asian Menu

A mix of red meat, seafood, and vegetables.

Grilled Beef Wraps with Fire Cucumbers and Ice Noodles (page 32)

Vietnamese Rice Noodle Rolls with Peanut Sauce (page 34)

Vietnamese Imperial Rolls with Nuoc Mam Sauce (page 35)

Spicy Pork-Filled Prawns with Lemon-Chili Dipping Sauce (page 37)

Italian Menu No. 1

From a variety of Italy's regions, a selection of hot, cold, simple, complex, hearty, and light appetizers combining vegetable-, meat-, seafood-, and bread- or pasta-based dishes.

Chicken-Coppa Rolls with Spinach (page 50)

Caponata Wrapped in Lettuce Leaves (page 53)

Herb-and-Garlic Bread Sticks (page 64)

Tomato-and-Ricotta–stuffed Manicotti with Pesto (page 66)

Fried Risotto-Ball Surprises (page 67)

Italian Menu No. 2

Figs, Roasted Red Peppers, and Parmesan Wrapped in Romaine Leaves (page 55)

Three-Meat-and-Cheese Bread Roll (page 58)

Prosciutto-Fontina Rolls with Tomato-Melon Chutney (page 61)

Smoked Ham and Brandy-Raisin Melon Wraps (page 65)

Middle Eastern Menu

A mix of Middle Eastern dishes, with an emphasis on vegetables.

Lamb-and-Feta–filled Grape Leaves (page 72)

Lentil-and-Pine-Nut–stuffed Eggplant (page 73)

Lebanese Lamb-and-Rice–stuffed Zucchini with Yogurt Sauce (page 74)

Hummus Pita Rolls with Cucumbers and Peppers (page 78)

Israeli Kibbeh Chalab (page 79)

Russian Menu

Two do-ahead appetizers and one last-minute assembly make this Russian menu perfect for a cocktail party.

Meat-and-Mushroom Piroshki (page 80)

Fish-and-Rice Rastegai (page 81)

Russian Caviar-stuffed Eggs (page 83)

Mediterranean Menu No. 1

Three dishes from the North African part of the Mediterranean.

Kibbeh (Meat-and-Onion–stuffed Cracked Wheat) (page 91)

Egyptian Lamb-and-Currant–stuffed Tomatoes (page 95)

Briouates with Assorted Fillings (page 96)

Mediterranean Menu No. 2

Three dishes from the southern European part of the Mediterranean.

Mediterranean Filo Rounds (page 87)

White Bean–stuffed Tomatoes (page 92)

Greek Dolmades (page 93)

Caribbean Menu

Three finger-food appetizers, perfect for casual entertaining. Substantial and hearty fare.

Caribbean Sweet Potato Balls (page 103)

Trinidadian Pork Pastelles (page 104)

Jamaican Beef Patties (page 105)

Latin American Menu

Four dishes from Mexico, Central and South America. The flautas and Chiles Rellenos are best served on plates before the main entree.

Peruvian Potato Balls with Pickled Vegetables (page 106)

Chicken-Chili Flautas with Guacamole (page 111)

Chiles Rellenos (page 114)

Corn-and-Cheese Quesadillas (page 115)

Cross-Cultural Menu No. 1

Finger food, casual and easy to prepare.

Chicken-and-Vegetable Mosaic (page 125)

Ham-and-Water-Chestnut Fried Wontons with Corn Relish (page 126)

Smoked Turkey–Three Pepper Rolls with Honey Mustard (page 131)

Cross-Cultural Menu No. 2

Elegant fish and seafood plate appetizers.
Smoked-Salmon-and-Potato–filled Sole with Lemon-Caper Sauce
(page 122)
Salmon-and-Chive Crepe Triangles with Two Caviars (page 128)
Shrimp-and-Scallop–filled Endive with Red Pearls and Aïoli (page 123)

EIGHT MIXED ETHNIC MENUS

Menu No. 1

Appetizers to prepare ahead and serve cold.
Tuna Tartare–stuffed Cucumbers (page 27)
Vietnamese Rice Noodle Rolls with Peanut Sauce (page 34)
Smoked Ham and Brandy-Raisin Melon Wraps (page 65)
Hummus Pita Rolls with Cucumbers and Peppers (page 78)
Greek Dolmades (page 93)
Chicken-and-Vegetable Mosaic (page 125)

Menu No. 2

Hot appetizers for a large party.
Burmese Samosas with Hot Chili Dipping Sauce (page 26)
Vietnamese Imperial Rolls with Nuoc Mam Sauce (page 35)
Three-Meat-and-Cheese Bread Roll (page 58)
Fried Risotto-Ball Surprises (page 67)
Steamed Cabbage Rolls with Smoked Chicken and Rice (page 129)

Menu No. 3

Mixed hot and cold finger appetizers.
Chinese Egg Rolls with Mustard Dipping Sauce (page 38)
Three Cheese–Walnut Pasta Wheels (page 64)
Meat-and-Mushroom Piroshki (page 80)
Vegetable-Olive–filled Filo Rolls (page 86)
Smoked Turkey–Three Pepper Rolls with Honey Mustard (page 131)

Menu No. 4

Elegant appetizers for a large party, to serve on a buffet table.

Spicy Pork-filled Prawns with Lemon-Chili Dipping Sauce (page 37)

Chicken-Coppa Rolls with Spinach (page 50)

Russian Caviar-stuffed Eggs (page 83)

Briouates with Assorted Fillings (page 96)

Smoked-Salmon-and Potato–filled Sole with Lemon-Caper Sauce
(page 122)

Shrimp-and-Scallop–filled Endive with Red Pearls and Aïoli (page 123)

Menu No. 5

Casual, simple appetizers.

Chinese Pot Stickers (page 44)

Hummus Pita Rolls with Cucumbers and Peppers (page 78)

Peruvian Potato Balls with Pickled Vegetables (page 106)

Chicken-Chili Flautas with Guacamole (page 111)

Corn-and-Cheese Quesadillas (page 115)

Menu No. 6

Do-ahead appetizers to serve at room temperature.

Tuna-Tartare–stuffed Cucumbers (page 27)

Roast Duck–Lettuce Packages with Apricot-Ginger Chutney (page 39)

Herb-and-Garlic Bread Sticks (page 64)

Greek Dolmades (page 93)

Menu No. 7

Do-ahead appetizers to serve at room temperature.

Vietnamese Rice Noodle Rolls with Peanut Sauce (page 34)

Chicken-Coppa Rolls with Spinach (page 50)

Caponata Wrapped in Lettuce Leaves (page 53)

Wild Mushroom–filled Pasta Shells (page 54)

Chicken-and-Vegetable Mosaic (page 125)

Menu No. 8

Appetizers to assemble ahead and cook in the oven just before serving.

Curried Malaysian Packets with Peanut Dipping Sauce (page 40)

Sausage-and-Cheese Mini Calzones (page 60)

Lentil-and-Pine-Nut–stuffed Eggplant (page 73)

Fish-and-Rice Rastegai (page 81)

III

Recipes

ASIAN

*T*he Asian tradition of eating many small meals and an endless supply of snacks makes this culture appear to be preoccupied with eating. When I visited Asia, it seemed to me that the entire population spent the major part of each day shopping for food, cooking, and eating! To say that most Asian people love to snack on small, savory tidbits throughout the day is an understatement. Because much of this eating is done on the streets, the food is portable, making it easy to eat on the run. Most of these appetizer-like foods are prepared by street vendors, but there are many shops that also prepare and sell bundles of ready-to-eat food. Soups, noodles, rice dishes, and banquet-style feasting is done in homes and formal restaurants, but snacking makes up the largest portion of everyday eating in many Asian countries.

Asian appetizers are perfect for serving at parties, because they are most often neat little bundles that include every taste, texture, color, and type of food imaginable—in one bite. Called *dim sum* in Chinese restaurants and *zensai* in Japan, foods that are served and eaten in small quantities before the main meal, or *as* the main meal, are plentiful and abundant. Street food in Southeast Asia can range from grilled meats, seafood, or poultry taken alone or wrapped in lettuce leaves; steamed yams or bananas; tropical fruits arranged on wooden sticks or packed in plastic bags; steamed or fried dumplings; rice noodle rolls filled with vegetables, meat, seafood, and fresh herbs; steamed buns stuffed with savory fillings; and fried pies served with spicy sauces. The variety of street-cooked food is staggering, and the skill and endurance of the cooks is amazing. This culture has perfected the take-away snack, and its cuisine is a lesson in economy, organization, culinary skill, and creativity.

Chinese, Vietnamese, Burmese, Japanese, Thai, and Malaysian dishes usually incorporate the freshest produce with small bits of meat, poultry, or seafood, using rice, noodles, or a combination of both as the binding, wrapping, or "holding" ingredient. These are perhaps the world's quintessential rolled, wrapped, and stuffed foods. They come in many forms: flaky stuffed pies; steamed pork buns; dumplings filled with myriad ingredients; fresh and lively rice noodle rolls; grilled meats, nuts, chilies, and fresh herbs wrapped in lettuce leaves; and stuffed prawns or squid. The combinations of ingredients are unique, and may seem foreign to a Westerner. Soy sauce, fermented black beans, chili paste, star anise, rice wine vinegar, bean curd, garlic, ginger, and a wild assortment of dried mushrooms and roots form the backbone of many Chinese dishes, while fresh mint, basil, cilantro, fish sauce, coconut, limes, chilies, and ground peanuts are common ingredients in Southeast Asian dishes. The Burmese and Malaysian cuisines are influenced by their surrounding countries and use all of the above ingredients, plus potatoes, in addition to the usual noodles and rice. Japanese cuisine depends greatly on soy and teriyaki sauces, dried bonito, dried and fresh seaweed or kelp, mirin, miso, sake, and myriad fresh and dried roots. While most of these Asian ingredients are used cross culturally, there are a few that distinguish one cuisine from another.

Asian food is known for being light, fresh, and low in calories and fat. Many of these appetizers are perfect served before a large Asian feast, but they also make outstanding hors d'oeuvres for a Western meal, or can be served as a sort of Asian antipasto meal. Don't worry about serving a Thai dish with a Chinese dish; they are all compatible and, combined properly, will make an exciting and flavor-packed meal.

Burmese Samosas
with Hot Chili Dipping Sauce

These crispy packages are served in Burmese homes as snacks or as appetizers for large family gatherings. I first had them in a San Francisco restaurant, and they were so delicious that I decided to make them at home. The filling is easy and simple, and although they are traditionally made with a homemade dough, I use Chinese egg roll skins instead. The fiery red dipping sauce adds heat to these savory packets. You will have to make the *samosas* in two batches, so either cook one batch at a time, or cook two batches using two large pans.

Makes about 24 packets

2 large baking potatoes, peeled and
    quartered
1 large onion, cut into small dice
4 garlic cloves, minced
¼ cup vegetable oil
1 tablespoon *each* ground coriander
    and ground turmeric
2 teaspoons caraway seed, ground
½ teaspoon ground mace

1 pound finely ground beef
1 bunch green onions, minced
One 2-inch piece fresh ginger, peeled
    and minced
3 tablespoons soy sauce
Salt and pepper to taste
3 tablespoons cornstarch
¾ cup water
12 egg roll skins
2 to 3 cups vegetable oil for cooking
Hot Chili Dipping Sauce, following

*C*ook the potatoes in salted boiling water to cover for 25 to 30 minutes, or until they are tender. Drain well and cool to room temperature. Cut into small dice and place in a large bowl.

In a large sauté pan or skillet, cook the onion and garlic in the ¼ cup of vegetable oil over moderately high heat, stirring from time to time, for 10 minutes, or until they are golden brown. Add the spices, herbs, and meat and cook over high heat for 2 to 3 minutes, stirring constantly. Add the green onions, ginger, and soy sauce and cook for 3 minutes. Add to the potatoes and mix well. Season with salt and pepper and refrigerate, covered, for 2 to 3 hours.

In a small bowl combine the cornstarch and the water, stirring to make a smooth emulsion. Lay several egg roll skins on a flat surface and cut in half across the diagonal, making 2 triangles. Brush the borders with the cornstarch slurry. Place about 1 tablespoon of filling at one corner of an egg roll skin, leaving ½-inch border, and fold the other side over to make a triangle shape. Seal the edges and refrigerate until ready to cook. Make all of the *samosas* in this fashion and refrigerate until ready to cook. Heat 1½ cups of the oil in a very large, heavy skillet over high heat. When the oil is hot, add a batch of the samosas and cook over high heat, turning the packets until golden brown on all sides, about 3 to 4 minutes. Remove with a slotted spatula and drain on paper towels. Place in a warm oven. Fill the skillet to the same level with new oil, and heat to the proper cooking temperature. Make the remaining samosas and serve immediately with the Hot Chili Dipping Sauce.

Hot Chili Dipping Sauce

4 red jalapeño chilies, stemmed and
chopped
3 garlic cloves, chopped
⅔ cup honey

2 tablespoons fresh lime juice
2 tablespoons soy sauce
Salt and pepper to taste

*P*lace all the ingredients except salt and pepper in a blender and puree until smooth. Season to taste and serve at room temperature. The sauce can be made ahead of time and stored, covered, in the refrigerator for 2 weeks.

Tuna Tartare–stuffed Cucumbers

This refreshing low-fat appetizer draws inspiration from Japanese cuisine. Stuffed cucumber rounds make excellent hot-weather appetizers, served with dry white wine or Asian beer.

Makes about 30 pieces

3 large English cucumbers
1¼ pounds fresh tuna, minced
Juice of 3 limes
¾ cup minced green onions

3 tablespoons prepared *wasabi* (Japanese horseradish)
Ground black pepper to taste
½ cup toasted pine nuts (see page 8)
3 tablespoons toasted or black sesame seeds (see page 8)

*S*lice the cucumbers into 1-inch rounds. Using a small spoon, gently scoop out the seeds, leaving a "bottom" in each piece of cucumber to hold the filling. Turn the cucumber cups upside down on paper towels to drain for about 20 minutes. Pat the inside of the cucumbers dry with clean, dry paper towels.

Combine the fish, lime juice, green onions, and *wasabi* in a small bowl; mix well and season with black pepper. Just before filling the cucumbers, add the pine nuts and sesame seeds to the fish mixture; mix well.

Carefully spoon some filling into each cucumber piece, making a dome of filling on the top of each piece. Serve chilled.

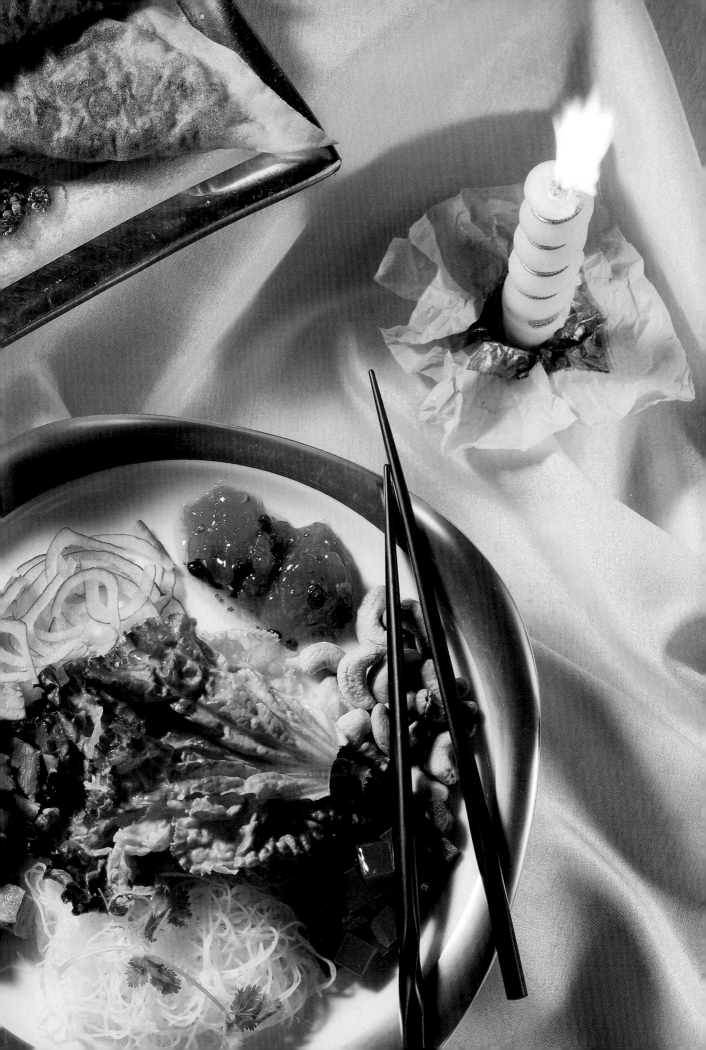

Thai Spicy Pork-and-Vegetable–stuffed Squid

Squid make the perfect container for a spicy mixture of ground pork, dried mushrooms, and carrots. Cleaning fresh squid is a bit time-consuming, but once you get the hang of it, the task is easy. These stuffed squid can be served whole for eating out of hand, or sliced to serve on small individual plates with the dipping sauce.

Makes 18 to 20 pieces

20 medium squid (about 2¼ pounds)
8 dried shiitake mushrooms
¾ pound finely ground pork shoulder
4 garlic cloves, minced
4 shallots, minced
1 large carrot, peeled and shredded

½ cup chopped fresh cilantro leaves
½ cup chopped fresh basil leaves
Juice of 2 limes
1 teaspoon *each* ground black pepper
  and salt
3 tablespoons vegetable oil
½ cup water
Spicy Dipping Sauce, following

To clean the squid: Cut the head (which is in the middle of the body) and tentacles from the body section, taking care not to break the ink sac (the ink is messy and will stain). Using your fingers, remove the spine and flesh from the inside of the body. Peel the thin, outer purple skin from the outside of the squid body. The squid body should now be a clean white tube, inside and out. Using a very sharp knife, prick the squid in 2 places, making a pin-sized hole. This will enable you to stuff the squid without forming air pockets. Set aside until ready to stuff.

Soak the mushrooms in warm water to cover for 15 to 20 minutes, or until they are soft and pliable. Remove the stems and slice the mushrooms into thin pieces. Place the mushrooms in a large bowl with the pork, garlic, shallots, carrot, cilantro, basil, lime juice, pepper, and salt; mix well.

Using your index finger, gently stuff each squid, packing the filling in and leaving about ½ inch of room at the top of each squid to allow for expansion. Using a very sharp knife, partially slice each stuffed squid several times across the body on the diagonal, making a ½-inch cut through to the filling. This will prevent the stuffing from coming out of the squid as it cooks.

Heat the oil in a very large sauté pan or skillet over moderate heat. Add the squid and cook for 1 minute, turning the squid so that all sides come in contact with the oil. Add the water and cook, covered, for 2 to 3 minutes, or until the squid is opaque and the filling is cooked. Remove from the pan and let sit at room temperature for 10 minutes. Serve at room temperature or, if serving sliced, refrigerate for 15 minutes before slicing into ¾- to 1-inch pieces. Serve with Spicy Dipping Sauce.

Spicy Dipping Sauce

2 tablespoons fresh lime juice
2 tablespoons fish sauce (*nuoc mam*)
3 garlic cloves

3 whole serrano chilies, stemmed
¼ cup chopped fresh cilantro
3 tablespoons corn syrup

*P*lace all the ingredients except the corn syrup in a blender. Puree until smooth and place in a small bowl. Add the corn syrup and mix well. Serve at room temperature. Store, covered, in the refrigerator for up to 1 week.

Thai Spinach Packages with Five Jewels and Chili-Honey Sauce

In this dish, inspired by a classic Thai appetizer, spinach leaves are filled with sweet, hot, sour, and salty flavors. To serve, place the bowls in the center of the table and let diners make their own packages as hot or pungent as they like. This is a very low-fat, low-calorie dish.

Makes 4 servings

Chili-Honey Sauce

¼ teaspoon dried red pepper flakes
1 red jalapeño chili, stemmed and
  minced
1 garlic clove, minced
¼ cup honey
Juice of 1 lime
1 tablespoon fish sauce (*nuoc mam*)

½ pound medium prawns
1 cup unsalted roasted peanuts
2 jalapeño chilies, stemmed, seeded,
  and cut into small dice
6 large garlic cloves, cut into small
  dice
30 very large spinach leaves, stemmed
  and washed

*C*ombine the sauce ingredients in a small bowl; mix well. Set aside at room temperature until ready to use.

Cook the shrimp in boiling water for 1 minute. Drain and immediately plunge them into ice water. Drain well. Remove the shells and tails and cut into ½-inch pieces. Place in a small bowl.

Place the roasted peanuts, jalapeño chilies, garlic, and bell pepper in separate small bowls. Stack the spinach leaves on a platter and surround them with the bowls of ingredients. Place the sauce in the center of the table. Take a spinach leaf in the palm of your hand and place a piece of shrimp and some peanuts, jalapeño chilies, garlic, bell pepper, and sauce in the center of the leaf. Wrap, dip, and eat!

Grilled Beef Wraps with Fire Cucumbers and Ice Noodles

This recipe uses some Japanese ingredients, but the idea comes from a traditional Thai appetizer. All the components can be prepared ahead of time, and each person makes his or her own packet at the table. The fork-tender grilled beef, combined with spicy cucumbers and cooling noodles and wrapped in crisp lettuce leaves, makes a wonderful summer appetizer. Miso is a paste made from fermented soybeans, and can be found in natural foods stores and Asian markets.

Makes about 20 rolls

Marinade

½ cup white miso paste
3 tablespoons sweet-hot mustard
¾ cup olive oil
⅓ cup teriyaki sauce
3 tablespoons apple cider vinegar
3 garlic cloves, minced
2 teaspoons ground black pepper

2 pounds filet mignon steaks
1 large English cucumber, halved, seeded, and thinly sliced

¼ cup seasoned rice wine vinegar
3 red jalapeño or serrano chilies, stemmed, seeded, and thinly sliced
1 small onion, thinly sliced
½ pound vermicelli noodles
⅓ cup sesame oil
⅓ cup black sesame seeds
½ cup chopped fresh cilantro leaves
⅓ cup chopped fresh mint leaves
Salt and pepper to taste
20 large green or red leaf lettuce leaves, washed and dried

*T*o make the marinade: Place the miso and mustard in a medium bowl. Slowly add the olive oil, whisking all the while to make a smooth emulsion. Add the teriyaki sauce and vinegar and continue whisking. Add the garlic and pepper and mix well. In a non-aluminum pan, marinate the steaks in the marinade for 2 days in the refrigerator, turning the meat every 8 hours so that all sides of the beef come in contact with the marinade. Remove the steaks from the refrigerator 2 hours before cooking.

Combine the cucumber, rice wine vinegar, red chilies, and onion in a bowl; mix well. Let the cucumbers stand at room temperature for 1 hour before serving. Prepare a fire in a charcoal grill.

Cook the noodles in boiling water until they are al dente, about 8 to 10 minutes. Drain well and place in a large bowl. Add the sesame oil, sesame seeds, cilantro, mint, salt, and pepper; mix well. Set aside at room temperature until ready to serve.

When the coals are red hot, that is, they have a thin layer of gray ash and are mostly red when tapped, place the steaks on the grill and cook on each side for 3 to 4 minutes, or until medium rare. Remove the steaks and let stand for 10 minutes before slicing. Slice into strips and place on a plate.

To assemble: Place a lettuce leaf in the palm of your hand. Put some noodles, cucumbers, and a few slices of meat in the center of the leaf, wrap the leaf around the filling, and eat.

Vietnamese Rice Noodle Rolls
with Peanut Sauce

These refreshing and healthful "rolled salads" are traditionally served as an appetizer before a Vietnamese meal. Rice paper and bottled hoisin sauce can be found in most Asian markets. Please refer to Basics (page 11) for notes on how to use this delicate rice paper.

Makes 14 to 16 rolls

1 pound pork tenderloin, trimmed of fat
32 small shrimp (about ½ pound)
¼ pound rice stick noodles
2 large carrots, peeled and shredded
1 tablespoon sugar
2 tablespoons fish sauce *(nuoc mam)*

Thirty-two 6-inch rice paper rounds (1 package)
4 cups water
8 large red or green leaf lettuce leaves, washed and patted dry
¾ cup fresh mint leaves
¾ cup fresh cilantro leaves
Peanut Sauce, following

*P*reheat the oven to 400° F. Place the pork loin on a roasting rack in a greased roasting pan. Roast for 15 to 17 minutes, or until the center is just barely pink. Remove from the oven and cool to room temperature. When cool enough to handle, cut the pork into paper-thin slices and set aside until ready to use.

Drop the shrimp into boiling water and cook for 30 seconds. Remove from the water and drop into cold water; drain well. When cool enough to handle, peel and remove the tails. Set the shrimp aside until ready to use.

Cook the noodles in boiling water for 2 to 3 minutes, or until they are tender but not mushy. Drain well and place in a bowl with the shredded carrots, sugar, and fish sauce. Mix well, using your hands, until all the ingredients are combined.

To assemble, work with only 2 sheets of rice paper at a time, and keep the large stack covered with barely damp towels to prevent the sheets from curling and drying out. Immerse 1 sheet of paper into a bowl filled with the water; quickly remove and place flat on a flat surface. The rice paper will become pliable in a few seconds. Immerse the second sheet in the same fashion and place on a flat surface, taking care not to let the 2 rice paper sheets touch.

Lay one half of a lettuce leaf across the bottom third of 1 rice paper. Place 1 tablespoon of the carrot-noodle mixture, 2 slices of pork, and several mint leaves in the center of the bottom third of the piece of lettuce. Gently roll the paper once over the filling and fold the sides in. Continue to fold halfway, making a tight package. Place 2 shrimp on the paper and top with a few cilantro leaves. Continue rolling, making a tight packet as you go. Wrap the roll in the second soaked and pliable rice paper, making a tight package. Place the rolls on a plate and cover with a damp towel so they will not dry out while you make the remaining rolls. Make the remaining rolls in the same fashion, working with only 2 sheets of rice paper at a time. To serve, cut in half and serve with the peanut sauce.

Peanut Sauce

1 tablespoon peanut oil
3 garlic cloves, minced
1 to 2 red jalapeño or serrano chilies,
  stemmed, seeded, and minced
½ cup water
1 tablespoon smooth natural peanut
  butter

½ cup hoisin sauce
Juice of 3 limes
¼ cup unsalted roasted peanuts,
  minced

*H*eat the oil in a small saucepan over moderate heat. When the oil is hot, add the garlic and chili and cook for 1 minute, stirring all the while. Add the water and bring to a boil. Add the peanut butter, hoisin sauce, and lime juice; mix well. Reduce the heat to low and cook for 3 to 4 minutes, stirring from time to time. Add the peanuts and cool to room temperature.

Vietnamese Imperial Rolls
with Nuoc Mam Sauce

These slender, crispy fried rolls are practically the national dish of Vietnam. They are usually served on special occasions, such as Vietnamese New Year, weddings, anniversaries, and festive banquets, and are available in most Vietnamese restaurants. They can be a bit tricky to assemble, but once you understand the rice paper and how it works, the results will be well worth the small effort. You can find rice paper and fish sauce, known as *nuoc mam*, in most any Asian market. Please read about deep-frying and working with rice paper in the Basics section (pages 5 and 11).

Makes about 12 rolls

Filling

6 dried shiitake mushrooms
¼ pound rice stick noodles
3 tablespoons fish sauce (*nuoc mam*)
5 shallots, minced
5 garlic cloves, minced
1 small carrot, peeled and shredded
¼ pound fresh cooked crab meat,
  picked over
½ pound raw shrimp, peeled, tails removed, and minced

¾ pound minced pork shoulder
¾ cup chopped fresh cilantro
1 teaspoon ground black pepper
Juice of 3 limes

6 cups water
¼ cup sugar
Twenty to twenty-five 6-inch rice
  paper rounds (1 package)
2 cups vegetable oil for cooking
Nuoc Mam, following

*S*oak the mushrooms in warm water to cover for 15 minutes. Drain and squeeze out the excess moisture with your hands. Remove the stems and slice the mushrooms into thin strips. Place in a large bowl.

Cook the noodles in boiling water for 2 to 3 minutes, or until tender but not mushy. Drain well and add to the mushrooms. Add the fish sauce, shallots, garlic, carrot, crab meat, shrimp, pork, cilantro, black pepper, and lime juice. Mix well, using your hands to combine all the ingredients. Refrigerate, covered, for at least 1 hour before assembling, or for up to 8 hours.

To assemble: Place the water and sugar in a very large bowl. Working with 2 sheets of rice paper at a time, keep the large stack covered with a barely damp cloth to prevent them from curling and drying out. Immerse the sheets, one at a time, into the sugar water, then quickly remove and place separately on a flat surface. Do not let the 2 sheets touch one another. The sheets will become pliable within seconds.

Place about 2 rounded tablespoons of filling along the bottom of the rice paper. Gently wrap the paper once over the filling, fold in the sides of the paper, and continue rolling, making a tight package. Set aside on a baking sheet in the refrigerator until ready to cook. Make the remaining rolls in this fashion and refrigerate until ready to cook.

Heat about 2 inches of the oil in a deep, heavy skillet over high heat. When the oil is hot but not smoking, add a small batch of the rolls and cook over high heat until they are golden brown on all sides, about 5 to 7 minutes. Remove with a slotted spatula and drain on paper towels. Place in a warm oven while cooking the remaining rolls. Slice into thirds and serve immediately with the sauce.

Nuoc Mam Sauce (Fish Sauce)

2 garlic cloves, minced

2 red jalapeño or serrano chilies, stemmed, seeded, and minced

2 tablespoons sugar

2 tablespoons water

2 tablespoons seasoned rice wine vinegar

¼ cup fresh lime juice

¼ cup *nuoc mam*

Combine all the ingredients and mix well. Seasoned rice wine vinegar can be found in all Asian markets and most natural and regular grocery stores. Serve at room temperature with Vietnamese Imperial Rolls.

Spicy Pork-filled Prawns
with Lemon-Chili Dipping Sauce

Thai people are fond of combining salty, sweet, sour, and hot flavors in one dish. This lean and bright-tasting meat and seafood dish is served in most Thai restaurants as an appetizer, but it also makes a nice lunch served with cold noodles or stir-fried vegetables.

Makes about 24 prawns

1 medium onion, cut into small dice
4 garlic cloves, minced
One 2-inch piece fresh ginger, peeled and minced
1 teaspoon dried red pepper flakes
1 tablespoon ground coriander
1 teaspoon caraway seeds, ground
3 tablespoons vegetable oil

1½ pounds ground pork shoulder
Grated zest of 1 lime
Juice of 2 limes
3 tablespoons fish sauce (*nuoc mam*)
¾ cup chopped fresh cilantro
1 large egg, lightly beaten
1 teaspoon ground black pepper
2 pounds jumbo prawns (about 24)
Lemon-Chili Dipping Sauce, following

*P*reheat the oven to 400° F. In a large sauté pan or skillet, cook the onion, garlic, ginger, red pepper flakes, and spices in the oil over moderate heat for 5 minutes, stirring frequently. Add the pork and cook for 1 minute, or until it *just* loses its pink color. Immediately remove from the heat, place in a large bowl, and cool to room temperature.

Add the lime zest, lime juice, fish sauce, cilantro, egg, and black pepper; mix well. Refrigerate, covered, for 2 hours, or up to 1 day before using.

Meanwhile, peel the prawns, leaving the tails intact (save the shells for making fish stock). Butterfly each prawn by carefully making a cut, from head to tail, down the center of the inner curve of each prawn. *Do not cut all the way through* the center of the prawns. You will need a flat surface for the stuffing, so do not cut the prawns in half.

Spread the prawns open so they are flat. Place about 1 to 2 teaspoons of filling on the cut side of each prawn, making a rounded top. Place the prawns on a lightly greased shallow baking pan and bake until the prawns are just opaque all the way through, about 5 to 7 minutes. Serve immediately with the Lemon-Chili Dipping Sauce.

Lemon-Chili Dipping Sauce

¼ cup fresh lemon juice
2 tablespoons honey
1 garlic clove

¼ cup unsalted roasted peanuts
1 or 2 red jalapeño or serrano chilies, stemmed and seeded

*P*lace all the ingredients in a blender. Puree until fairly smooth. Serve at room temperature.

Chinese Egg Rolls with Mustard Dipping Sauce

This is a classic Chinese appetizer in America. Simple to make and easy to serve, these savory deep-fried rolls get an extra punch from a dash of Chinese hot chili sauce. You may serve them with the suggested Mustard Dipping Sauce, or your favorite hoisin or plum sauce.

Makes 16 egg rolls

Filling

6 large dried shiitake mushrooms
¾ pound ground pork shoulder
2 tablespoons rice wine or dry sherry
1½ tablespoons cornstarch
3 tablespoons sesame oil
4 garlic cloves, minced
1¼ cups shredded green cabbage
1 bunch green onions, minced
1 cup fresh bean sprouts

1 medium carrot, peeled and shredded
1 to 2 teaspoons Chinese hot chili sauce
Ground black pepper to taste

3 tablespoons cornstarch
½ cup water
16 egg roll wrappers (about ½ package)
2 to 3 cups vegetable oil
Mustard Dipping Sauce, following

*S*oak the mushrooms in warm water to cover for 15 minutes. Drain and squeeze the excess water from the mushrooms. Remove the stems and cut the mushrooms into thin slices. Set aside.

In a small bowl, combine the pork, rice wine, and cornstarch. Let sit at room temperature for 20 minutes.

Heat the sesame oil in a large sauté pan or skillet. When the oil is hot, add the pork and cook over high heat for 2 to 3 minutes or until it has lost its pink color. Add the garlic, cabbage, and green onions and cook over high heat for 2 minutes. Remove from the heat and add the bean sprouts, carrot, and mushrooms; mix well and season with hot chili sauce and black pepper. Refrigerate, covered, for at least 2 hours or up to 1 day.

In a small bowl, combine the cornstarch and water; mix well. Lay several wrappers on a flat surface. Place about 2 rounded tablespoons of filling along the bottom of 1 wrapper. Roll once, enclosing the filling, and fold in the sides of the wrapper. Roll, making a tight cylinder. Brush the edge of the wrapper with the cornstarch wash and finish rolling, making a tight seal. Refrigerate the finished egg rolls while you make the remaining rolls.

Heat about 2 cups of the oil in a very large, heavy saucepan. When the oil is very hot (see page 5), add the egg rolls in batches. Cook over high heat until golden brown on all sides, about 2 to 3 minutes. Remove with a slotted spoon and drain on paper towels. Serve immediately with the Mustard Dipping Sauce.

Mustard Dipping Sauce

⅓ cup powdered Chinese mustard

⅓ cup water

3 tablespoons sherry vinegar

2 tablespoons soy sauce

1 garlic clove, minced

*I*n a small bowl, combine the mustard, water, sherry vinegar, and soy sauce to make a smooth paste. Add the garlic and mix well. Let sit for at least 1 hour at room temperature before serving. You may need to thin the mustard after it sits. Add more water and stir to make a smooth paste.

Roast Duck–Lettuce Packages with Apricot-Ginger Chutney

This is a variation on a classic Thai appetizer that combines dried shrimp, peanuts, silver noodles, hot chilies, and fresh herbs, all wrapped in a lettuce leaf package. The chutney can be made 5 days ahead and stored in the refrigerator until ready to use. You can use a good commercial chutney if you are short on time.

Makes about 18 packets

Chutney

1 small onion, cut into small dice

3 garlic cloves, minced

2 jalapeño chilies, cut into small dice

One 2-inch piece fresh ginger, peeled and minced

1 teaspoon ground coriander

½ teaspoon *each* ground mace, ground cardamom, and ground black pepper

3 tablespoons vegetable oil

2 cups coarsely chopped fresh apricots

3 tablespoons fresh lime juice

¼ cup water

3 tablespoons currants

Salt and pepper to taste

2 Moscovy duck breast halves (2 pounds total)

1 small onion, sliced paper thin

½ cup roasted cashew nuts

1 medium red bell pepper, stemmed, seeded, and cut into small dice

½ pound thin cellophane noodles, cooked and drained

½ cup fresh cilantro leaves

18 medium green or red leaf lettuce leaves, washed and dried

*T*o make the chutney: In a large sauté pan or skillet, cook the onion, garlic, jalapeño chilies, ginger, and spices in the oil over high heat for 5 minutes, stirring often. Add the apricots, lime juice, water, and currants and bring to a boil. Reduce the heat and cook over moderate heat for 30 minutes, stirring often. Taste and add salt and pepper. Let cool and store in the refrigerator in a covered container for up to 3 weeks.

Preheat the oven to 400° F. Prick the skin of the duck breasts and place them in a roasting pan, skin side up. Roast for 15 to 20 minutes, pricking the skin every 5 minutes. Remove from the oven and let stand for 10 minutes before cutting. Cut into ½-inch chunks and place in a bowl.

Place the onion, nuts, pepper, noodles, and cilantro in separate small bowls.

Arrange the lettuce leaves on a large platter and serve the duck, chutney, and other condiments with the lettuce leaves.

To serve: Place a few pieces of duck, some cashews, red peppers, some noodles, onion, cilantro, and a bit of chutney inside a lettuce leaf; wrap and eat!

Curried Malaysian Packets with Peanut Dipping Sauce

These delicious savory pies are sold by street vendors throughout Malaysia. The fillings vary, but I especially enjoyed this one while traveling in Penang. The peanut sauce is terrific with the packets, but is not a necessary accompaniment, and the filling is best if made one day ahead.

Makes about 24 packets

Dough

1¾ cups unbleached all-purpose flour
1 teaspoon salt

½ teaspoon ground coriander
4 tablespoons unsalted butter, cut into 8 pieces
¼ cup vegetable oil
½ cup cold water or more

Filling

1 medium onion, cut into small dice
4 garlic cloves, minced
One 2-inch piece fresh ginger, peeled and minced
1 jalapeño chili, stemmed, seeded, and minced
2 teaspoons ground coriander
1 teaspoon ground turmeric
½ teaspoon *each* mace and cumin

1 teaspoon *each* fennel and caraway seed, ground
3 tablespoons vegetable oil
¾ pound finely ground pork shoulder
2 tablespoons fresh lime juice
Salt and pepper to taste

1 quart vegetable oil for cooking
Peanut Dipping Sauce, following

*T*o make the dough: Combine the flour, salt, and coriander in a medium bowl. Add the butter and mix with your hands until the mixture resembles coarse meal. Add the vegetable oil and mix until it is just incorporated. Add ½ cup water, mixing with your hands and gathering the dough into a ball as you go. If the dough does not form a ball, add 1 or 2 more tablespoons of water. Gather the dough into a ball, place on a lightly floured surface, and knead for 1 to 2 minutes. Wrap in plastic and store in the refrigerator overnight, or let rest at room temperature, loosely covered with plastic wrap, for 1 hour.

Place the dough on a lightly floured surface and divide the dough into 4 equal balls. Divide each ball again into 4 equal balls and flatten into disc shapes. Roll each disc out into a circle about 2 ½ inches across. Cover with plastic until ready to fill.

To make the filling: in a large sauté pan or skillet, cook the onion, garlic, ginger, jalapeño, spices, and herbs in the oil over moderate heat for 10 minutes, stirring often. Add the meat and lime juice and cook over high heat for 3 to 4 minutes. Season with salt and pepper and let cool.

Place about 1½ rounded tablespoons of filling at the bottom of each circle, leaving about a ½-inch border. Brush the edges with water and fold over, making a half-circle shape. Seal with the tines of a fork. Repeat to fill all the circles. Cover with a towel and refrigerate for at least 1 hour before cooking.

Heat about 2 inches of oil in a very large, heavy saucepan. When the oil is hot, add the packets in batches and cook until golden brown on both sides, about 4 to 5 minutes. Drain on paper towels and keep warm in a low oven if not serving immediately. Serve the packets on a large platter, with the peanut sauce in a small bowl.

Peanut Dipping Sauce

¾ cup coconut milk

½ cup chunky peanut butter

3 garlic cloves, minced

½ teaspoon dried red pepper flakes

¼ cup soy sauce

¼ cup fresh lime juice

Salt and ground white pepper to taste

*P*lace all the ingredients in a small bowl and mix well. Serve at room temperature. The sauce will thicken as it stands.

A Note on Coconut Milk: You can find coconut milk in Latin, Indian, Middle Eastern, Caribbean, Asian, and natural food stores and most large grocery stores. It's very time consuming and difficult to make at home.

Chinese Steamed Pork Buns

Traditionally served as part of a dim sum meal, these savory buns are easy to make and serve. They are perfect for parties, as they can be eaten out of hand and do not require a sauce. Typically, roast pork is used for the filling, but in this recipe, chopped pork and spices are cooked together, so that the flavors truly marry. The filling is best if made a day ahead. You can find all the ingredients for this dish in most grocery stores and Asian markets.

Makes 24 buns

¾ pound pork shoulder, minced
3 tablespoons sesame oil
5 garlic cloves, minced
One 3-inch piece fresh ginger, peeled and minced
1½ tablespoons five-spice powder

1 tablespoon Szechwan peppercorns, crushed
½ cup soy sauce
1½ cups dry red wine
¼ cup oyster sauce
5 large green onions, minced
½ cup hoisin sauce
1 tomato, minced

Dough

5 cups unbleached all-purpose flour
3 tablespoons sugar
2 teaspoons salt

1 package (2½ teaspoons) active dry yeast
2 cups warm (105° to 115° F) water

*T*o make the filling: In a large saucepan, cook the pork in the sesame oil over moderate heat for 3 to 4 minutes, or until the meat loses its pink color. Add the garlic, ginger, five-spices, and pepper and cook for 2 minutes over high heat, stirring all the while. Add the soy sauce, wine, and oyster sauce and reduce the heat to moderate. Cook over moderate heat for 1 hour, or until the meat is very tender and the sauce is thick. Add the green onions, hoisin sauce, and the tomato, and cook for 3 to 4 minutes. Set aside until ready to use, or refrigerate overnight.

To make the dough: Place the flour, sugar, and salt in a large bowl; mix well. Dissolve the yeast in the water, stirring with a spoon. Slowly add the water and yeast to the dry ingredients, stirring with your hands as you go. Form the dough into a ball. If the dough needs more water, add just enough to make it gather into a ball. If the dough is too sticky, add a little more flour, just enough to make it workable.

Gather the dough into a ball and place on a lightly floured surface. Knead the dough for about 5 minutes, or until it is smooth and elastic.

Place the dough in an oiled, clean bowl and turn to coat, cover with a damp cloth or plastic wrap, and place in a warm place to rise. When the dough has doubled in size, in about 1½ to 2 hours, remove it from the bowl and knead on a lightly floured surface for 3 to 4 minutes.

Divide the dough into 24 equal balls. Cover with a damp cloth and let it rest for 15 minutes. Flatten each ball into a disc about 2 inches in diameter. Place about 1 tablespoon of filling in the center of the dough. Wrap the dough around the filling, sealing and twisting the edges as you go. Place the bun on a square of waxed paper and set aside until ready to cook. Make all the buns in this fashion.

Fill a large wok half full of water. Bring to a boil over high heat. Place the buns (still on the waxed paper) on the tray of a bamboo steamer, leaving ½ inch of space between each bun. You will need to use both layers of the steamer, if possible, and, depending on the size of your steamer, you may have to cook the buns in 2 batches. Cover the steamer with the lid and cook over high heat for 10 to 12 minutes. Remove from the steamer and serve immediately.

Chinese Pot Stickers

This popular northern Chinese lunch dish is a winning appetizer found on most every Chinese menu in the United States. Legend has it that pot stickers were invented by accident. The emperor's chef mistakenly forgot the meal on the stove, and cooked the bottom of the tender dumplings, turning them golden brown. Pot stickers are traditionally eaten with a combination of hot chili oil, soy sauce, and rice vinegar, but are wonderful without any condiments. Cook half the pot stickers at a time, or use two very large pans and cook two batches at the same time.

Makes about 32 pot stickers

1 pound freshly ground pork shoulder
4 garlic cloves, minced
5 green onions, minced
One 2-inch piece fresh ginger, peeled and minced
3 tablespoons soy sauce

2 tablespoons sesame oil
1 teaspoon ground black pepper
1 teaspoon salt
3 tablespoons cornstarch
2 to 3 cups water
1 pound (32) 1½-inch pot sticker skins (about 1 package)
¼ cup vegetable oil

*I*n a large bowl, combine the pork, garlic, green onions, ginger, soy sauce, sesame oil, black pepper, and salt; mix well.

In a small bowl, combine the cornstarch and water, and mix to make a smooth emulsion. Lay several pot sticker skins out on a flat surface. Brush the edges with the cornstarch slurry. Place 1 rounded teaspoon of filling on one side of a skin, leaving a ¼-inch border. Fold over and seal the edges. Make "pleats" around the edge by folding over tiny sections of the sealed edge to form a "ruffled" border. The pot sticker should be flat on the underside and rounded on the top. Make all of the pot stickers in this fashion and refrigerate them for at least 1 hour or up to 4 hours before cooking.

To cook 1 batch of pot stickers: Heat 2 tablespoons of the oil in a 12-inch nonstick sauté pan or skillet over high heat. When the oil is hot, add a batch of pot stickers and cook over high heat for 2 to 3 minutes, or until the bottoms are golden brown. Reduce the heat to low (it is important to reduce the heat before adding the water so that the hot oil does not ignite), add 1 cup of cold water, cover, and bring to a boil over high heat. Reduce the heat to moderate and cook, covered, until most of the liquid has evaporated, about 5 to 7 minutes. Remove the cover and cook until the liquid evaporates, the bottoms are crisp, and the top dough is cooked. Place in a warm oven while cooking the second batch. Serve immediately.

Mu Shu Pork

I will never forget the first time I had mu shu pork in a Chinese restaurant in San Francisco. A Chinese friend of mine urged me to try this Asian "burrito," made with a filling of sautéed pork, black mushrooms, eggs, and green onions. A delicate pancake, spread with plum sauce, makes the perfect wrapper for the savory filling. You can buy a hoisin or plum sauce in the Asian section of your grocery store, or in an Asian market, but I think the plum sauce recipe here is better than the store-bought variety. I have included a recipe for the pancakes, or wrappers, but if you are short on time, you can use 6-inch flour tortillas instead.

Makes about 16 packages

Pancakes

1 cup unbleached all-purpose flour

¼ cup plus 2 tablespoons boiling
  water

3 tablespoons vegetable oil

¾ cup oil for cooking

Filling

¾ pound lean pork loin, cut into
  julienne

3 tablespoons soy sauce

2 tablespoons dry sherry

2 tablespoons cornstarch

6 dried shiitake mushrooms

4 dried cloud ear mushrooms (about 1
  ounce)

2 tablespoons vegetable oil

1 large bunch green onions, cut into
  1-inch lengths

5 garlic cloves, minced

5 eggs, lightly beaten

Plum Sauce, following

*T*o make the pancakes: Place the flour in a medium bowl. Slowly add the boiling water and 3 tablespoons of the oil, stirring as you add the liquids and mixing to form a dough. Gather the dough into a ball and turn out onto a flat surface. Knead for about 5 minutes, cover with plastic wrap or a damp cloth, and let sit at room temperature for 30 minutes to 1 hour. On a lightly floured surface, divide the ball into 16 equal-sized balls. Flatten each ball into a disc shape, and roll it out into a circle about 7 inches in diameter.

Heat 1 teaspoon of the oil in an 8-inch nonstick sauté pan or skillet. When the oil is hot, add a pancake and cook over low heat until it just starts to bubble on the surface. Flip over and cook on the second side until it is just barely golden brown. If you overcook the pancakes they will be too brittle to wrap around the filling; they should be very soft and flexible, like crepes. Make all the pancakes in this fashion, using oil as needed, and set them aside, covered with plastic wrap, until ready to use.

To make the filling: Marinate the meat in the soy sauce, sherry, and cornstarch at room temperature for 30 minutes. Meanwhile, soak the mushrooms in warm water to cover for 15 to 20 minutes, or until they are soft and pliable. Drain the mushrooms, squeezing out excess water with your hands, and remove the stems. Cut the mushrooms into very thin strips and set aside until ready to use.

Heat the oil in a very large sauté pan, skillet, or wok over very high heat. When the oil just begins to smoke, add the garlic and green onions. Cook over high heat for 30 seconds. Remove from the pan and set aside. Add the meat and cook over high heat for 1 to 2 minutes, or until the meat just loses its pink color. Add the green onions and garlic, mushrooms, and eggs. Cook over moderately high heat for 1 to 2 minutes, or until the eggs are just set. Remove from the pan and place on a large platter with the pancakes. Serve immediately with the plum sauce.

Plum Sauce

2 tablespoons sesame oil
4 garlic cloves, minced
One 2-inch piece fresh ginger, peeled
   and minced

¼ cup black rice or balsamic vinegar,
   or red wine
¾ cup plum preserves or jelly
½ cup hoisin sauce

Heat the oil in a saucepan over high heat. When the oil is hot, but not smoking, add the garlic and ginger and cook over moderate heat for 2 minutes, stirring all the while. Add the vinegar, preserves, and hoisin sauce. Bring to a boil over high heat, reduce the heat to low, and simmer for 10 minutes. Remove from heat and cool to room temperature. Store in the refrigerator for up to 2 weeks.

ITALIAN

The traditional Italian meal is divided into several courses, the first one being the antipasto course. Antipasto, meaning "before the meal," consists of a vast assortment of little dishes including grilled vegetables, fried risotto balls, marinated squid, cured meats, and fruit and cheese. In Italy, this course is particularly popular in restaurants, where large carts or tables groaning with an array of unique and tempting dishes are displayed in the entryway of the dining rooms. Antipasto carts are wheeled to individual tables so that diners can choose their favorite dishes. Antipasto is not commonly served for everyday meals in most Italian homes, but for large family gatherings and holiday celebrations you will see grand platters of food passed at the table.

Italian cuisine is flexible in that many larger dishes can be made smaller, making them more appropriate for pre-dinner appetizers. This is the case with Sausage-and-Cheese Mini Calzones (page 60), and the Wild Mushroom–filled Pasta Shells (page 54). Both of these would normally be served as a main dish, but when pared down to a smaller size and served before the main meal, they make perfect appetite teasers. Fried Risotto-Ball Surprises (page 67) and Smoked Ham and Brandy-Raisin Melon Wraps (page 65) are classic Italian antipasto dishes, and are ideal for cocktail parties, as they are easy to eat out of hand. Chicken-Coppa Rolls with Spinach (page 50) and Goat Cheese–Pasta Rounds (page 68) draw inspiration from Italian ingredients and cooking methods, but were created for this book. Grilled Radicchio with Goat Cheese and Sun-Dried Tomatoes (page 62); Figs, Roasted Peppers, and Parmesan Wrapped in Romaine Leaves (page 55); and Caponata Wrapped in Lettuce Leaves (page 53) are contemporary Italian dishes, a little lighter and a bit more visually pleasing than some of the more traditional antipasto dishes. They are perfect as small tastes before dinner or, even better, served on one large platter at an informal Italian feast.

While many of these recipes are rich and filling, they all can be served in small portions before a meal, or combined and served as one large meal (see Menus, page 15). Preparing many small dishes ahead of time can make entertaining a more relaxing and soothing experience, rather than one filled with a lot of last-minute details, cooking, and tension. The

Italian tradition of antipasto comes from a love and passion for food, drink, good conversation, and hours spent sitting around a dinner table. This can be a lively way to entertain guests, or a simple way to have a family meal. Either way, one or two small antipasto dishes can elevate the most humble meal to an unforgettable event, and creatively combining several antipasto dishes for one lusty feast can make for a truly successful dinner party.

Chicken-Coppa Rolls
with Spinach

These colorful bite-sized rolls are easy to prepare and can be made up to two days ahead and stored in their cooking liquid. Coppa is a spicy cured meat made from pork, and can be found in Italian delis and many grocery stores. Serve the rolls with Tomato Relish, following, for an elegant presentation.

Makes about 25 pieces

1 large onion, cut into small dice

5 garlic cloves, minced

½ cup olive oil

1 teaspoon *each* dried thyme, oregano, and basil

3 large bunches fresh spinach, stemmed and washed

Salt and pepper to taste

2 whole boned chicken breasts with skin (1 pound each)

½ pound thinly sliced hot coppa

3 cups chicken stock or broth

Tomato Relish, following

*P*reheat the oven to 400° F. In a large sauté pan or skillet, cook the onion and garlic in 5 tablespoons of the olive oil over moderately high heat for 10 minutes, stirring frequently. Add the herbs, reduce the heat to low, and cook until the onions are soft, about 5 to 7 minutes.

Chop the spinach coarsely. Add the spinach to the onions and garlic and cook over high heat until just wilted, about 1 minute. Immediately remove from heat and season with salt and pepper. Let cool.

Place the chicken breasts skin side up on a flat surface. Using a rolling pin or mallet, flatten to a thickness between ¼ and ½ inch taking care not to rip or tear the skin. Turn the breast over so that the skin side is down and the long side is towards you.

Divide the coppa in half and cover each breast with slices of coppa, leaving a 1-inch border. Place half of the spinach mixture along the bottom of the long end of each breast. Roll once, enclosing the spinach mixture inside the breast, and fold the sides of the chicken in. Continue to roll tightly. Make the other chicken roll in the same fashion.

Place the remaining 3 tablespoons of olive oil in a 9-by-15-inch baking pan. Place in the oven for 5 to 7 minutes. Remove the pan from the oven and place the chicken rolls seam side down in the hot oil. Bake for 5 minutes. Cover with the chicken stock or broth and aluminum foil, and cook an additional 12 to 15 minutes. Remove from the oven and remove the chicken rolls from the cooking liquid with a slotted spoon, reserving the cooking liquid. Set the rolls aside on a cutting board to cool. If serving within the hour, cover and refrigerate the rolls until ready to serve. If serving more than 2 hours later or the next day, store the cooled rolls in the cooled liquid until ready to serve. When rolls are cool and firm, drain if necessary, and slice into ½-inch rounds. Reserve the cooking liquid for another use.

Tomato Relish

1 large onion, cut into small dice
2 garlic cloves, minced
¼ cup olive oil
1 teaspoon fennel seeds

6 Roma tomatoes, peeled, seeded, and
   finely chopped
½ cup chopped fresh basil leaves
Salt and pepper to taste

*I*n a heavy skillet or saucepan, cook the onion and garlic in the olive oil over moderate heat for 10 minutes, stirring frequently. Add the fennel seeds and tomatoes and stir well. Cook over moderate heat for 10 minutes, add the basil, and remove from heat. Season with salt and pepper and serve alongside the chicken rolls.

Caponata Wrapped
in Lettuce Leaves

This mélange of Mediterranean vegetables is excellent spread on bread or served as a side dish to roasted lamb or chicken. Find oil-cured olives in an Italian, Greek, or natural foods store, or substitute Kalamata olives. This dish is best if made a day ahead.

Makes about 20 packets

2 large onions, cut into small dice
6 garlic cloves, minced
⅓ cup fruity olive oil
1 medium eggplant, cut into small dice
2 teaspoons *each* dried thyme, oregano, basil, and marjoram
1 teaspoon dried red pepper flakes
2 celery ribs, cut into small dice

1 zucchini, cut into small dice
½ cup balsamic vinegar
1½ cups chopped peeled and seeded tomatoes (about 2 large tomatoes)
½ cup chopped pitted green olives
½ cup chopped pitted oil-cured black olives
3 tablespoons capers, drained
Salt and pepper to taste
20 large green leaf lettuce leaves, washed and dried

*I*n a large sauté pan or skillet, cook the onions and garlic in the olive oil over moderate heat for 15 minutes, stirring from time to time. Add the eggplant, herbs, and red pepper flakes and cook for 10 to 15 minutes, or until the eggplant is almost tender.

Add the celery, zucchini, and balsamic vinegar and cook over high heat for 5 minutes, stirring constantly. Add the tomatoes and reduce the heat to moderately low. Cook for 20 minutes, or until the mixture is thick and soft. Add the olives and capers and mix well. Season with salt and pepper and cool to room temperature.

Place 1 to 2 tablespoons of caponata in each lettuce leaf and fold the bottom of the leaf over the filling; fold in the sides and continue to roll the leaf. Serve at room temperature.

Wild Mushroom–filled
Pasta Shells

Bite-sized, rich, and bursting with mushroom essence, these easy-to-assemble pasta shells also make an excellent main dish, served with a light tomato sauce. Almost any wild mushroom in season will add the right texture and flavor, but if you can't find any, use cultivated mushrooms. South American dried mushrooms are an excellent and inexpensive substitute for precious Italian dried porcini. Both kinds can usually be found at a natural foods, specialty, or Italian food market. A small amount of oil added to the pasta water coats the shells with enough oil to keep them moist but not oily.

Makes about 25 shells

½ pound large pasta shells
3 tablespoons vegetable oil
2 ounces dried porcini mushrooms
1 large onion, cut into small dice
4 garlic cloves, minced
1 tablespoon rubbed dried sage
2 teaspoons dried thyme
½ cup olive oil
½ cup Madeira wine
¾ pound cultivated mushrooms,
  halved and sliced

3 tablespoons unsalted butter
¼ pound chanterelles, oyster mushrooms, or other wild mushrooms,
  coarsely chopped
¼ pound shiitake mushrooms,
  stemmed and cut into medium slices
¼ pound Parmesan cheese, grated
2 cups crème fraîche or sour cream
Salt and pepper to taste
¼ cup minced fresh parsley or sprigs
  of flat-leaf parsley for garnish

*C*ook the pasta shells in a large pot of salted boiling water with the vegetable oil until they are al dente, about 10 to 12 minutes. Drain and plunge them into cold water. When the shells are cool, drain and set them aside on paper towels, gently separating any that have stuck together. Cover with a damp towel until ready to use. Before filling the shells, pat the interiors dry with a towel.

Soak the dried mushrooms in warm water to cover for 20 to 25 minutes, or until the mushrooms are tender. Drain and cover with clean water. Using your hands, remove any grit or sand from the mushrooms. Drain and clean again. Slice the mushrooms and rinse with clean cold water.

In a large sauté pan, cook the onion, garlic, and herbs in ¼ cup of the olive oil over moderate heat for 10 to 15 minutes, or until the onion is golden brown. Add the Madeira and cook over moderate heat until the liquid evaporates, about 2 minutes. Remove from the pan and place in a large bowl.

Using the same pan, heat a thin layer of oil over high heat. Add the cultivated mushrooms and cook over high heat, stirring frequently, until they are golden brown and have lost their moisture, about 5 to 7 minutes. Add to the onions.

Heat the remaining oil and the butter in the same pan and cook the remaining mushrooms over moderate heat until they are tender, about 5 minutes. Add to the onion-mushroom mixture along with the dried mushrooms and Parmesan cheese. When the mixture is cool, add the crème fraîche or sour cream and mix well. Season with salt and pepper.

Fill each shell with the mushroom mixture and garnish with minced parsley or a sprig of flat-leaf parsley. Serve at room temperature.

Figs, Roasted Red Peppers, and, Parmesan Wrapped in Romaine Leaves

This is surely one of the easiest finger-food appetizers to prepare. If you are really pressed for time, you can buy marinated roasted peppers at an Italian deli or grocery store. Each diner makes his or her own package filled with sweet, salty, and peppery ingredients. If you cannot find the superior imported Parmesan cheese called Reggiano, substitute imported Grana Padano or Asiago cheese.

Makes 15 packages

2 red bell peppers
3 tablespoons fruity olive oil
1 garlic clove, minced
Salt and pepper to taste

15 large romaine lettuce leaves, washed and patted dry
16 to 20 dried black Mission figs, stemmed and sliced
⅓ pound Parmesano Reggiano cheese, sliced thin or cut into chunks

*R*oast the peppers as described in Basics, page 6; stem, peel, seed, and slice the roasted peppers. Combine the roasted pepper slices, olive oil, garlic, salt, and pepper in a small bowl; mix well.

Place the lettuce leaves on a large platter. Place the remaining ingredients in small individual bowls. Take a lettuce leaf in your hand and fill the center, along the rib, with some figs, roasted peppers, and a bit of cheese. Fold into a long tube and eat!

Three-Meat-and-Cheese Bread Roll

Sausage-and-Cheese Mini Calzones

Prosciutto-Fontina Rolls with Tomato-Melon Chutney

Figs, Roasted Red Peppers, and Parmesan Wrapped in Romaine Leaves

Three-Meat-and-Cheese Bread Roll

There are several traditional Italian bread rolls that date back to ninth-century Sicily. They are usually formed into a crescent shape, but it is not imperative that you bake yours in this fashion. These ingredients vary slightly from the classic bread roll, but I find them to be just as good, if not better. This rich and flavor-packed appetizer is even better the next day.

Makes 16 to 20 servings

2 recipes Basic Bread Dough, page 12

Filling
1 large onion, cut into small dice
5 garlic cloves, minced
¼ cup olive oil
2 teaspoons dried basil
1 teaspoon dried rosemary
1 pound sweet Italian sausage, removed from casings
1 bunch Swiss chard, stemmed and chopped

½ pound sliced hot coppa
½ pound sliced smoked ham
½ pound smoked mozzarella cheese, cut into small dice
1 pound Fontina cheese, cut into small dice
Salt and pepper to taste

1 recipe Parsley-Oregano Pesto, following (optional)
Olive oil for brushing

*P*repare the bread dough and let rise. Meanwhile, make the filling. In a large sauté pan or skillet, cook the onion and garlic in the olive oil over moderate heat for 15 minutes, stirring frequently, until golden brown. Add the herbs and sausage, and cook for 5 to 7 minutes. Add the Swiss chard and cook until the greens just wilt, about 3 to 4 minutes. Drain the mixture for 15 minutes, then place in a large bowl and let cool to room temperature. Add the coppa, ham, and cheeses to the cooked mixture. Mix well and season with salt and pepper. Divide the filling in half.

Preheat the oven to 350° F. Divide the risen dough in half. On a lightly floured surface, roll each piece of bread dough into a rectangular shape between ¼ and ½ inch thick. Place the dough so that the long side is towards you. If using the pesto, spread half of the Parsley-Oregano Pesto on one piece of bread dough, leaving a 1-inch border. Spread the remaining pesto on the other piece of dough.

Spread half of the filling over each piece of bread dough, leaving a 1½-inch border. Roll each piece tightly, taking care to keep the filling inside. Do not tear the bread dough, or the filling will run while baking. Pinch the ends like a sausage to enclose the filling and place each roll on a lightly greased jelly roll pan. Brush each roll all over with olive oil. Bake for 15 minutes and brush with more olive oil. Continue baking for about 1 hour, or until rolls are golden brown. Remove from the oven and let cool for 30 minutes before slicing.

Parsley-Oregano Pesto

1½ cups packed fresh parsley sprigs
¼ cup packed fresh oregano leaves
¾ cup olive oil
2 tablespoons sherry vinegar

¼ cup pine nuts
1 garlic clove
2 ounces Parmesan cheese, grated
1 tablespoon water (optional)
Salt and pepper to taste

*P*lace all the ingredients except the water and salt and pepper in a blender and puree until smooth. Add the water if necessary. Season with salt and pepper. Cover and refrigerate until ready to use. Store in the refrigerator for up to 3 days.

Sausage-and-Cheese
Mini Calzones

If you are pressed for time, make the filling a day ahead, and leave the dough and the assembly for the next day. These are a bit tedious to make, but they make perfect hand-held appetizers. To shorten the assembly time, make the dough circles twice as large, for more traditional-sized calzones. This savory, robust filling makes an excellent pizza topping.

Makes about 24 small calzones

2 recipes Basic Bread Dough, page 12

Filling
6 tablespoons fruity olive oil
¾ pound mushrooms, halved and sliced
1 pound whole-milk ricotta cheese (about 2 cups)
½ pound Fontina cheese, grated
¼ pound Parmesan cheese, grated
1 cup fresh basil leaves, coarsely chopped

1 large onion, cut into medium dice
6 garlic cloves, minced
2 teaspoons fennel seed
2 teaspoons *each* dried basil, oregano, rosemary, and thyme
1 pound hot Italian sausage, removed from casings and crumbled
Salt and pepper to taste

1 egg yolk, beaten
Fine cornmeal (optional)
Olive oil for brushing

*P*repare the dough and let rise once. Divide it in half, cover with a towel, and let rest at room temperature until it does not spring back when poked with a finger, about 20 minutes. On a lightly floured surface, divide each half into 12 balls and flatten into disc shapes. Cover with a damp towel and let rest for 20 minutes at room temperature.

Meanwhile, make the filling: Heat 2 tablespoons of the olive oil in a large non-stick sauté pan or skillet. When the oil is hot but not smoking, add the mushrooms and cook over high heat, stirring frequently, until they are golden brown and have lost all their moisture, about 5 minutes. Remove from the pan and place in a large bowl. When the mushrooms are cool, add the ricotta, Fontina, Parmesan cheese, and basil; mix well.

In a clean sauté pan or skillet, cook the onion, garlic, and spices in the remaining 4 tablespoons of the olive oil over moderate heat for 10 minutes, stirring frequently. Add the sausage and cook until it loses its pink color, about 5 or 6 minutes. If the mixture is very fatty, drain in a colander for 1 minute. (Some fat and juice are necessary for flavor and moisture.) Cool to room temperature and add to the mushrooms and cheese. Mix well and season with salt and pepper.

Preheat the oven to 450° F. Preheat a pizza stone in the oven, if you have one. Roll each dough disc into a 3½-inch round. Brush the edge of the circle with the egg yolk. Place about 1½ to 2 tablespoons of filling on one half of each circle, leaving a ½-inch border. Fold the other half of the dough over the filling, but do not stretch or overfill the dough. Gently roll the edges together, sealing them tightly.

Place the calzones on a preheated pizza stone or on a baking sheet sprinkled with fine cornmeal. Brush the calzones with olive oil and bake for 10 minutes. Remove from the oven and, using a very sharp knife, pierce the top of each calzone 2 or 3 times (this allows steam to escape and encourages the filling to remain inside the dough). Reduce the temperature to 400° F and bake, brushing from time to time with olive oil, until golden brown, about 50 minutes. Serve immediately, or reheat the next day in a preheated 350° F oven for 10 to 15 minutes.

Prosciutto-Fontina Rolls
with Tomato-Melon Chutney

Salty prosciutto, creamy Italian cheese, and sweet-hot chutney team up in this simple hors d'oeuvre. Substitute Bel Paese or Tallegio for the Fontina if you prefer a more flavorful cheese. The sweet-hot chutney takes on a golden hue with the addition of the orange-colored melon. It is also good spread on crackers or bread.

Makes about 20 rolls

Tomato-Melon Chutney
1 large onion, cut into small dice
2 garlic cloves, minced
3 tablespoons olive oil
2 medium tomatoes, peeled, seeded, and chopped
⅓ cup dry sherry
1 cup finely chopped cantaloupe

2 teaspoons dried red pepper flakes
¼ cup minced fresh parsley
Salt and pepper to taste

½ pound prosciutto (about 20 slices)
¾ pound Italian Fontina cheese, cut into ¼-inch julienne
20 leaves fresh basil, washed and dried

To make the chutney, in a large sauté pan or skillet, cook the onion and garlic in the olive oil over moderate heat for 10 minutes, stirring frequently. Add the tomatoes, sherry, cantaloupe, and red pepper flakes and cook over high heat for 3 minutes. Reduce the heat to moderate and cook for 10 to 15 minutes, stirring from time to time. Add the parsley and cook for 3 to 4 minutes. Season with salt and pepper, and set aside at room temperature until ready to use.

To make the rolls, lay each slice of prosciutto on a flat surface. Place a piece of cheese, a basil leaf, and about 1 teaspoon Tomato-Melon Chutney at the short end of each slice of meat. Roll, keeping the filling enclosed. Serve at room temperature.

Grilled Radicchio with Goat Cheese and Sun-Dried Tomatoes

These rolls can be almost finger size, depending on the shape of each radicchio leaf. The slightly bitter flavor of this gorgeous red leafy vegetable is the perfect foil for rich goat cheese and piquant sun-dried tomatoes. If you cannot find radicchio, use cabbage or jarred grape leaves.

Makes about 22 rolls

22 large radicchio leaves (3 large heads radicchio)
1 cup coarsely chopped drained sun-dried tomatoes

2 garlic cloves, minced
¾ cup toasted pine nuts (see page 8)
¾ pound mild goat cheese
¼ pound Parmesan cheese, grated
Black pepper to taste

*P*repare a fire in a charcoal grill. Core each head of radicchio by removing the center core with a paring knife. Do not cut the leaves of the radicchio.

Bring a large pot of water to boil over high heat. When the water is boiling, add 4 or 5 of the radicchio leaves. Blanch for 1 second, immediately remove them from the water, and plunge them into cold water; drain. Blanch all the leaves in batches of 4 or 5. Remove the hard stem by cutting a ½-inch triangle of core from the center of each leaf. This will facilitate rolling and make the finished texture more pleasing. Dry the leaves by rolling them between layers of paper towels.

In a large bowl, combine the sun-dried tomatoes, garlic, pine nuts, goat cheese, and Parmesan cheese; mix well. Season with black pepper and refrigerate for 30 minutes to 1 hour.

Place a radicchio leaf on a flat surface, core-end towards you. Place 1½ to 2 teaspoons of filling, depending on the size of the leaf, at the bottom of the leaf. Roll once, fold the sides of the leaf in, and continue to roll, making a tight, neat packet. Make all the stuffed radicchio leaves in this fashion and refrigerate until ready to use.

When the coals are medium hot, place the radicchio packets on the grill and cook for 2 to 3 minutes, rotating constantly. The cheese should be hot and creamy, and the leaves should be a bit darker and almost crisp in places. Serve immediately.

Herb-and-Garlic Bread Sticks

This may be stretching the rolled, wrapped, and stuffed theme of this book, but these wound bread sticks are irresistible. Fresh and still warm from the oven, they are wonderful by themselves, and make a nice accompaniment to salads, soups, or antipasto plates.

Makes about 20 bread sticks

1½ cups unbleached bread flour
½ teaspoon salt
1 tablespoon cracked black pepper
1¼ teaspoons active dry yeast
½ cup warm (105° to 110° F) water

1 cup fruity olive oil
6 garlic cloves, minced
2 tablespoons *each* minced fresh
   thyme and oregano
1 tablespoon minced fresh rosemary
Kosher salt for sprinkling

*P*lace the flour, salt, and pepper in a large bowl; mix well. Dissolve the yeast in the water and stir to form a paste. Add 3 tablespoons of the olive oil and mix well. Add this mixture to the dry ingredients, stirring with your hand or a wooden spoon to form a dough. The dough should be soft but not sticky. If the dough is too dry, add a little more water, just enough so that the dough gathers into a ball. If the dough is too sticky, add just enough flour to make it easy to handle. Gather the dough into a ball and turn out onto a lightly floured surface. Knead the dough for about 5 minutes, or until it is elastic and smooth. Place in a lightly greased bowl, turn to coat the dough with grease, and cover with a damp cloth or plastic wrap. Let rise in a warm place until doubled in size, about 1½ hours.

Remove the dough from the bowl and knead on a lightly floured surface for 2 minutes. Cover with a damp cloth and let rest for 20 to 25 minutes. Meanwhile, preheat the oven to 450°. Preheat a pizza stone in the oven, or if you are not using a pizza stone, preheat a heavy sheet pan.

In a small bowl, combine the remaining olive oil, garlic, and herbs. Roll out the dough to a thickness of about ¼ inch. Brush the dough with the garlic oil and cut it into 1-inch-wide strips. Fold each strip in half the long way, so that the oiled surfaces come together. Twist the strips, making long, thick ribbons about ½ inch wide. Place the ribbons on the preheated stone or the oiled baking sheet and brush liberally with the garlic oil. Bake for 5 minutes, remove from the oven, and brush again with the garlic oil. Continue baking for 5 to 7 minutes, or until the bread sticks are golden brown on all sides. Brush with the oil one last time, sprinkle with Kosher salt, and serve warm.

Three Cheese–Walnut Pasta Wheels

The luscious combination of three cheeses, crunchy walnuts, and fresh basil wound inside lasagne noodles makes a stunning appetizer. The wheels are also excellent served with a light tomato sauce for dinner.

Makes about 30 wheels

1 pound lasagne noodles (preferably with ruffled edges)
1 large onion, cut into small dice
4 garlic cloves, minced
3 tablespoons olive oil
⅓ pound Parmesan cheese, grated

⅓ pound Gorgonzola cheese
1¼ pounds whole-milk ricotta cheese
½ cup toasted walnuts (see page 8)
⅓ cup chopped fresh basil leaves
½ teaspoon fennel seed, ground
¼ teaspoon grated nutmeg
Salt and pepper to taste

*C*ook the pasta in a large pan of boiling salted water over moderately high heat for 8 to 10 minutes, or until the noodles are al dente. Do not overcook the noodles or they will break apart. Carefully drain the noodles, and gently remove one at a time, placing each noodle flat on an oiled baking sheet. Brush the tops lightly with oil and cover with a damp cloth until ready to use.

In a large sauté pan or skillet, cook the onion and garlic in the olive oil over moderate heat for 10 minutes, or until the onions are golden brown. Place in a large bowl and cool to room temperature. Add the Parmesan and Gorgonzola cheese and mix well. Add the ricotta cheese and mix well. Add the remaining ingredients and mix well. Cover and refrigerate for at least 3 hours or up to 2 days.

To assemble: Place 1 noodle on a flat surface, short side towards you. Wipe off any excess oil with a clean cloth or paper towels. Spread 3 or 4 tablespoons of filling over the noodle, making a smooth surface. Roll, keeping the filling inside the noodle. Fill and roll all the noodles in this fashion. Cover tightly with plastic wrap and refrigerate for at least 2 hours or up to 1 day. Using a very sharp knife, slice each roll in half, making 2 half pinwheels, and serve at room temperature.

Smoked Ham
and Brandy-Raisin Melon Wraps

Aside from soaking the raisins, this simple dish takes only a few minutes to prepare, and is a wonderful way to showcase the sweet and juicy melons of summer.

¾ cup golden raisins
1 cup brandy
¾ pound thinly sliced smoked ham

1 small honeydew melon, peeled and sliced into ½ inch wide wedges

*S*oak the raisins in the brandy for 2 to 3 hours. Drain and reserve the brandy for another use. Place 1 slice of ham on a flat surface. Place 4 or 5 raisins on one end of the ham slice, cover with a slice of melon, and wrap, keeping the raisins against the melon and the ham and allowing the ends of the melon to be exposed. Make all the melon wraps in this fashion. Serve on a large platter or individual plates at room temperature.

Tomato-and-Ricotta–stuffed
Manicotti with Pesto

This rich appetizer also makes a simple light supper, served with a vegetable or green salad. Feel free to substitute your favorite tomato sauce for the pesto.

Makes 14 rolls

Pesto

1½ cups packed fresh basil leaves
¾ cup olive oil
2 garlic cloves

2 ounces Parmesan cheese, grated
¼ cup pine nuts
Juice of 1 lemon
Salt and pepper to taste

Filling

30 ounces fresh whole-milk ricotta
   cheese
⅓ pound Asiago cheese, grated
¾ cup sun-dried tomatoes, drained
   and minced
1 bunch chives, minced
1 teaspoon anise seed

¼ teaspoon grated nutmeg
3 medium tomatoes, cut into small
   dice
Salt and pepper to taste

14 manicotti shells
3 tablespoons olive oil

*P*reheat the oven to 400° F. To make the pesto: Place all the ingredients in a blender and puree until smooth. You may need to add a tablespoon of water or so, if the pesto seems too thick. Place in a bowl and cover with plastic until ready to use, or refrigerate, covered, for up to 3 days. Remove the pesto from the refrigerator 1 hour before serving.

Combine the ricotta cheese, Asiago cheese, sun-dried tomatoes, chives, anise seed, and nutmeg in a bowl; mix well. Add the tomatoes, salt, and pepper and mix gently.

Cook the manicotti shells in salted boiling water for 10 to 12 minutes, or until al dente. If the pasta is overcooked, the tubes could break and then would not be usable. Drain and pat dry with paper towels, taking care not to tear or break the shells.

Using a pastry bag without a tip, fill each shell with some of the filling, taking care, once again, not to break or tear the pasta shells. Place in a lightly greased baking pan, leaving about ¼ inch between each shell (for easy removal). Brush the shells with the olive oil and bake for 10 to 15 minutes, or until the rolls are just warmed through. You may also serve the rolls unbaked, at room temperature. Drizzle the pesto over the rolls to serve.

Fried Risotto-Ball Surprises

These irresistible golden brown nuggets are a bit time-consuming to make, but they are well worth the effort. It is best to make the risotto a day ahead, leaving only the assembly and the cooking for the last minute.

Makes about 80 balls

Risotto

1 large onion, cut into small dice
2 garlic cloves, minced
5 tablespoons unsalted butter
1½ cups Arborio rice
1 teaspoon *each* dried thyme, oregano, rosemary, and sage
4 to 5 cups chicken stock or broth at room temperature

⅓ pound Parmesan cheese, grated
Salt and pepper to taste

½-inch-thick slice smoked ham (about ½ pound), cut into ½-inch cubes
3 large eggs, lightly beaten
2 cups finely ground dry bread crumbs
2 to 3 cups light olive or vegetable oil for cooking

To make the risotto: In a large, heavy pot, cook the onion and garlic in the butter over moderately low heat for 10 minutes, stirring from time to time. Add the rice and herbs, and cook over moderate heat for another 2 minutes, stirring constantly. Add 2 cups of the chicken stock or broth and bring to a boil. Reduce the heat to moderately low and cook, uncovered, until the liquid is absorbed into the rice, stirring from time to time. Add 2 more cups of the stock or broth and cook in the same fashion. When all the liquid has been absorbed, taste the rice and test for doneness. The rice should be slightly chewy, but not underdone. If the rice needs more cooking, add the last cup of stock or broth and cook until it is absorbed. Remove from the heat and add the cheese, mix well, and season with salt and pepper. Refrigerate, covered, for at least 6 hours or for up to 2 days.

To make the balls: Place about 1 tablespoon of risotto in the palm of your hand. Place 1 cube of ham in the center of the rice, enclosing the ham completely. Make sure the ham is completely covered. Make all the balls in this fashion and refrigerate for 1 hour.

In batches, roll the balls in the beaten eggs, taking care to cover them completely. Dredge in the bread crumbs, covering them, once again, completely. Place the rolled balls on a baking sheet covered with bread crumbs. Repeat to coat all the balls.

Heat about 2½ inches of oil in a heavy skillet over moderately high heat. When the oil is hot but not smoking, add the balls in batches and cook, turning them until they are golden brown on all sides. Make all the risotto balls in this fashion, removing each batch with a slotted spoon and draining them on paper towels. Keep the cooked balls warm in a low oven while you cook the entire batch. Serve immediately.

Goat Cheese–Pasta Rounds

I developed this recipe one evening when I had leftover pasta. It makes a rich and satisfying appetizer, or can be served along with a green salad for a light supper or lunch.

Makes 8 to 10 servings

¾ pound thin spaghetti
4 garlic cloves, minced

1 medium onion, thinly sliced
Salt and pepper to taste
½ cup olive oil

Filling

¼ pound cream cheese
½ pound goat cheese
¾ cup chopped fresh basil leaves
¾ cup coarsely chopped drained sun-dried tomatoes

1 tomato, finely diced
Salt and pepper to taste
Fresh basil sprigs for garnish

Cook the spaghetti in a large pot of salted boiling water until al dente. Remove from the water and drain. Place in a large bowl and mix with the garlic, onion, salt, pepper, and olive oil. Refrigerate, covered, for 2 hours or up to 1 day.

Divide the pasta in half. Heat a 12-inch nonstick sauté pan or skillet over moderate heat. Add half of the pasta and cook over moderately high heat until golden brown on one side, about 7 to 10 minutes. Carefully flip the "pancake" over by sliding it onto a large plate and returning it to the skillet, uncooked side down. Cook the second side until it is golden brown. Remove from the pan and set it aside on a flat surface. Cook the remaining pasta in the same manner and cool on a flat surface.

To make the filling, combine the goat cheese, cream cheese, basil, and sun-dried tomatoes in a bowl; mix well. Add the fresh tomato and mix gently. Season with salt and pepper.

Spread the filling on one of the pasta rounds. Top with the second round and gently press to secure. Slice into triangles and serve at room temperature. Garnish with sprigs of fresh basil.

MIDDLE EASTERN
AND RUSSIAN

*J*n the Middle East, the assortment of small plates of food served with drinks, or before the main course are called *mezze*. This extremely popular custom is a great way to enjoy many tastes, textures, and ingredients, and has been part of life in this part of the world since the dawn of recorded culinary history. The Russians have two great food ceremonies: the Russian tea ceremony, and the *zakuski,* or hors d'oeuvre ceremony. The latter is most often a lavish offering of a grand assortment of small plates of food, served with iced vodka. This custom is thought to have originated in the days when country estates were far apart, and traveling guests would arrive hungry and in need of libation. Although the upper class managed to produce most any type of food for these extravagant buffets, modest households served more humble fare in a more informal style.

The foods of the Middle East are often highly spiced, but not hot and fiery as are many Asian dishes. Lamb is the most popular meat, and while grains play an important part in this diet, they are usually combined with some sort of vegetable or meat and are rarely served as a side dish. The different cuisines of this area have similar styles of preparing foods, but each country enjoys a unique and separate cuisine. Stuffed vegetables are common, but even more popular are filled grape leaves. Savory flavors are often combined with sweet, and when hot chilies are used, there is always a cooling sauce, perhaps made from yogurt, to put out the fire. Pine nuts, walnuts, pistachios, and almonds are used both in savory dishes as well as sweet, and an abundance of dried fruit is used in many Middle Eastern dishes.

Two of the appetizers in this section are really plate appetizers, and could be served on a buffet table along with other multiethnic appetizers. The most common *mezze* served in the Middle East are not rolled, wrapped, or stuffed, and can be rather plain in comparison to the recipes included here. Lamb-and-Feta-filled Grape Leaves is not a traditional Middle Eastern dish, but one that takes inspiration from these wonderful ingredients. The same goes for the Hummus Pita Rolls with Cucumbers and Peppers. This healthy dish combines several classic Middle Eastern ingredients in a contemporary, easy-to-serve fashion. All of these dishes would be good served with an assortment of flavorful imported olives, and perhaps Armenian cracker bread.

Russian *zakuski* can include a multitude of small dishes, but the key "ingredient" is vodka. Traditionally, the participant—and we can use that word here because this custom is as much theater-of-the-dining-room as it is a meal—is seated at the table and proceeds to empty the contents of a very small special glass of vodka into his or her mouth without pausing. This spine-tingling moment can be followed by a slice of pickled or creamed herring, a slice of dark bread with cheese and radish, caviar, sliced meat, or smoked sturgeon or salmon. Even the most humble homes serve a wide variety of food for pre-dinner snacking. Wild game and fowl; marinated mushrooms; sliced meats; cheeses; pickled vegetables; smoked and fresh fish; stuffed tomatoes or peppers; tomato, onion, and cucumber salads; and an array of prepared fish, cabbage, and potato salads are standard fare. By the early 1800s, it became fashionable to serve *zakuski* on a separate buffet table in a separate room, where diners could help themselves to the many different plates of food. In a less formal situation, the *zakuski* would be presented in the center of the dining table, where the plates would be passed around the table to each diner. Restaurants generally serve the appetizers one at a time to each diner at the table.

The Russian appetizers that appear in this book are, of course, either rolled, wrapped, or stuffed. Eastern Europeans are known for their small savory pies and turnovers, called *piroshki, rastegai, piroghi,* or *vatroushkai.* These can be made with yeasted or non-yeasted doughs, and are filled with sweet cheese, cottage cheese, meats, fish, potatoes, and vegetables, or sometimes poultry. They can be served alone, with pickled vegetables, or as a garnish for soup. Both the *piroshki* and the *rastegai* are simple and easy to prepare, and are delicious served with iced vodka, or a robust beer or ale.

Lamb-and-Feta–filled
Grape Leaves

Stuffed grape leaves are a traditional Middle Eastern appetizer or main dish, and whether they are stuffed with rice, meat, or a combination of both, they make perfect little packages for serving at parties. Feta cheese and red peppers are not traditionally used in most Middle Eastern fillings, but they add flavor, texture, and richness to these savory appetizers, which are best if made a day ahead.

Makes 30 to 35 pieces

One 8-ounce jar grape leaves, packed
   in brine
1 large onion, cut into small dice
4 garlic cloves, minced
3 tablespoons olive oil
2½ pounds lamb, shoulder or stew
   meat, chopped coarse (not ground)
1 tablespoon ground coriander

1 teaspoon fennel seed
1 teaspoon cumin seed
½ cup dry red wine
2 cups beef broth
1 red bell pepper, stemmed, seeded,
   and cut into small dice
½ pound feta cheese, crumbled
Juice of 2 lemons
Salt and pepper to taste

*D*rain the grape leaves and carefully separate them. Using kitchen scissors, snip the tough stem from each leaf. Rinse with cool water, pat dry with paper towels, and set aside until ready to use.

In a large sauté pan, or skillet, cook the onion and garlic in the olive oil over moderate heat for 10 minutes. Add the lamb and herbs and cook over high heat for 5 minutes, stirring frequently. Add the wine and cook until all the liquid has evaporated. Add the broth and bring to a boil. Reduce the heat and cook over moderately low heat until the meat is very tender, about 45 to 50 minutes. Add the bell pepper and cook until it is tender, about 3 minutes. Cool to room temperature. Add the cheese, lemon juice, salt, and pepper; mix well and set aside.

Preheat the oven to 400° F. Lay the grape leaves, dull side up, on a flat surface. Place about 1 teaspoon of filling along the bottom of each leaf. Roll once, turn in the sides of the leaf, and continue wrapping to form a very tight roll, but taking care not to tear the leaf. Stuff all the grape leaves in this fashion.

Place the stuffed grape leaves in a greased shallow baking pan. Cover with aluminum foil and bake for 10 to 15 minutes. Remove from the oven and cool to room temperature.

Lentil-and-Pine-Nut–stuffed Eggplant

Middle Easterners are fond of stuffing almost any vegetable with a savory filling of meat, vegetables, nuts, or a combination of all three. Silky soft eggplant and a crunchy grain-and-vegetable filling make these Middle Eastern appetizers pleasing to even the most ardent meat-and-potato fan. Choose long narrow purple Japanese eggplants, or small white Thai eggplants. If the only eggplant available is the large Western variety, go ahead and make this satisfying dish, slicing the finished product into individual portions.

Makes 12 pieces

6 Italian, Japanese, or Chinese eggplants
Olive oil for cooking
1 large onion, cut into small dice
4 garlic cloves, minced
¼ cup fruity olive oil
2 teaspoons *each* ground coriander, and cumin
2 teaspoons anise seed, ground
½ teaspoon *each* ground cinnamon, mace, and cardamom
¾ cup lentils, washed and sorted
3 cups water, chicken stock, or chicken broth
1 tomato, cut into small dice
1 cup minced fresh parsley
¾ cup toasted pine nuts
Salt and pepper to taste
Olive oil and/or fresh lemon juice for drizzling (optional)

*P*reheat the oven to 400° F. Slice each eggplant in half lengthwise and rub it all over with olive oil. Place cut side down on a baking sheet and bake for 15 to 20 minutes, or until the inside is soft. Remove from the oven and let cool to room temperature. When the eggplant is cool enough to handle, gently scoop out the flesh, leaving a ¼-inch shell and taking care not to tear or break the skin. Place half of the pulp in a medium bowl and reserve the rest for another use. Set the pulp aside until ready to use.

In a large, shallow saucepan, cook the onion, garlic, and spices in the ¼ cup olive oil over moderate heat for 10 minutes, stirring frequently. Add the lentils and the water, stock, or broth and bring to a boil. Reduce the heat and cook over moderate heat for 40 to 45 minutes, or until the lentils are soft but not mushy. Add the tomato and cook over high heat for 3 to 4 minutes without stirring, until the lentils are very aromatic and the bottom layer is brown. Remove the lentils from the pan and add to the eggplant pulp. Add half of the parsley and all of the pine nuts and mix well. Season with salt and pepper.

Spoon the filling into the eggplant shells, taking care not to break the shells. Garnish with the remaining chopped parsley and, if you wish, drizzle the tops with olive oil and/or lemon juice.

Lebanese Lamb-and-Rice–stuffed Zucchini with Yogurt Sauce

A spicy lamb, rice, and pistachio nut stuffing makes these filled zucchini very satisfying. Meat-and-rice stuffed vegetables are traditionally served as part of a Middle Eastern dinner, but this one can be served as an appetizer or even as a light lunch.

Makes 10 pieces

5 medium zucchini
½ cup white long-grain rice
3 cups water
1 large onion, cut into small dice
4 garlic cloves, minced
3 tablespoons vegetable oil
½ pound ground lamb

1 tablespoon ground coriander
2 teaspoons ground cumin
1 teaspoon *each* ground cinnamon, allspice, and black pepper
1 large tomato, finely chopped
¾ cup toasted shelled pistachio nuts (see page 8)
Salt and pepper to taste
Yogurt Sauce, following

*P*reheat the oven to 400° F. Cook the zucchini in salted boiling water for 3 minutes. Drain and let cool to room temperature. When cool enough to handle, slice in half lengthwise. Using a small spoon, carefully remove the flesh of the zucchini, leaving a ¼-inch shell and taking care not to break or tear the outside of the zucchini. Reserve the pulp for another dish. Drain the hollowed-out zucchini, cut side down, on paper towels for 30 to 45 minutes.

Place the water in a large saucepan and bring to a boil over high heat. Add the rice and cook over high heat for 15 to 20 minutes, or until tender but not mushy. Drain well and place in a large bowl; set aside.

In a large sauté pan or skillet, cook the onion and garlic in the oil over moderate heat for 10 minutes, stirring frequently. Add the lamb, herbs, and spices and cook over high heat for 3 minutes, stirring constantly. Add the tomato and cook for about 5 minutes, or until the mixture is thick and the tomato has broken down. Let cool to room temperature and add the pistachio nuts. Combine with the rice; mix well and season with salt and pepper.

Fill the cavity of each zucchini with about 2 rounded tablespoons of filling, patting it in as you go. Place in a lightly greased baking pan and bake, covered, for 10 to 15 minutes, or until the filling is hot. Remove from the oven and serve with the yogurt sauce.

Yogurt Sauce

1 cup plain yogurt
2 garlic cloves, minced

¼ cup minced fresh mint
½ teaspoon cayenne pepper

*C*ombine all the ingredients in a small bowl; mix well. Chill for 1 hour before serving. Store, covered, in the refrigerator for up to 3 days.

Koftas (Indian Meatballs)

I can't omit my favorite Indian meatballs, even though they don't fit into the Middle Eastern or Russian category. These spicy, golden brown meatballs have a surprise stuffing of garlic, chilies, and ginger. They are traditionally served with a tomato-based sauce as an entree, but the smaller size used in this recipe, and the cooling yogurt dipping sauce, make them perfect before-dinner snacks.

Makes about 30 small meatballs

Meatballs
2 pounds finely ground lamb
1 tablespoon ground coriander
2 teaspoons ground black pepper

1 teaspoon *each* ground cloves, fenugreek, cumin, fennel, star anise, and cardamom
1½ teaspoons salt
1 egg, lightly beaten

Stuffing
3 jalapeño or serrano chilies, stemmed, seeded, and minced
3 garlic cloves, minced
One 1-inch piece fresh ginger, peeled and minced

1 tablespoon fresh lime juice
1 quart vegetable oil for deep-frying

Yogurt Dipping Sauce, following

*I*n a large bowl, combine the ground lamb, spices, herbs, salt, and egg; mix well. Refrigerate, covered, for at least 2 hours.

In a small bowl, combine the stuffing ingredients and mix well. Set aside until ready to use.

To make the meatballs: Using a tablespoon as a measure, divide the mixture into 30 balls. Take 1 ball in the palm of your hand and, using a finger moistened with water, make a hole in the center of the ball. Place about ¼ teaspoon of filling in the hole and close the meat around it, making a tight ball. Make all the meatballs in this fashion, and refrigerate until ready to cook.

Heat the oil over high heat in a heavy 3-quart pot. When the oil is hot, add a small batch of meatballs and cook over high heat for 2 to 3 minutes, or until the meatballs are golden brown on all sides. Remove with a slotted spoon and drain on paper towels. Keep the cooked meatballs in a warm oven. Cook the remaining meatballs in this fashion, taking care not to crowd them. Serve immediately with the Yogurt Dipping Sauce.

Yogurt Dipping Sauce
1½ cups plain yogurt
2 garlic cloves, minced
½ cup finely chopped cilantro

¼ cup finely chopped fresh mint
Salt and pepper to taste

*C*ombine all the ingredients in a small bowl; mix well. Serve slightly chilled. Store, covered, in the refrigerator for up to 3 days.

Hummus Pita Rolls
with Cucumbers and Peppers

Creamy hummus and crisp vegetables team up to make a refreshing, yet satisfying bite-sized appetizer. This vegetarian Middle Eastern–inspired dish is easy to prepare. Use very fresh pita breads, or they may be difficult to roll.

Makes 12 rolls

3 cups cooked chick-peas (garbanzo beans)

⅔ cup tahini (ground Middle Eastern sesame paste)

6 to 8 garlic cloves

¾ to 1 cup olive oil

Juice of 6 lemons

Salt and pepper to taste

6 very fresh 8-inch whole-wheat pita breads, split in half to make 12 *rounds*

1 large English cucumber, cut into slices 5 inches long and ¼ inch thick

1 long red sweet pepper

1 long yellow sweet pepper

Leaves from 1 small bunch fresh mint

*P*lace the chick-peas, tahini, garlic, ¾ to 1 cup of olive oil, and lemon juice in a blender or food processor. Puree until smooth. Season with salt and pepper.

Spread the inside of each pita bread with about 2 tablespoons of hummus, leaving a 1-inch border. Place a couple of slices of each vegetable and a few leaves of mint at one end of a pita bread, making a tight bundle. Roll, enclosing the vegetables. Fill and roll all the pita rolls in this fashion. Slice into 1-inch rounds and serve at room temperature.

Israeli Kibbeh Chalab

This is an updated and livelier version of a very old Hebrew dish. These flat potato-and-rice cakes, filled with chicken meat and livers, use Middle Eastern spices and are wonderful served with olives, pickled vegetables, or hot pepper sauce.

Makes about 22 to 24 cakes

3 cups dry mashed potatoes (5 to 6 potatoes)
1½ cups cooked white rice
2 hard-cooked eggs, coarsely chopped
1 egg, lightly beaten
Salt and pepper to taste
1 medium onion, cut into small dice
3 tablespoons chicken fat or vegetable oil

4 whole chicken livers, coarsely chopped
2 teaspoons *each* ground cumin, cardamom, and fennel seed
1 teaspoon ground mace
1 cup minced cooked chicken meat
Salt and pepper to taste
1½ cups finely ground dry breadcrumbs
Olive oil for cooking

*I*n a large bowl, combine the mashed potatoes, rice, hard-cooked eggs, uncooked egg, salt, and pepper, and mix well. Refrigerate, covered, for 2 to 3 hours, or up to 1 day.

In a large sauté pan or skillet, cook the onion in the chicken fat or vegetable oil over moderate heat for 15 minutes, stirring from time to time. Add the livers, herbs, and spices and cook for 4 to 5 minutes, or until the livers are just cooked. Remove from the pan and place in a bowl along with the cooked chicken meat. Mix well and season with salt and pepper.

Lightly dust your hands with flour to prevent the dough from sticking. Place about 2 rounded tablespoons of the potato-rice mixture in the palm of your hand. Make a hole in the center of the mixture with your finger, and fill with about 1½ teaspoons of filling. Enclose the ball and flatten slightly to make a cake. Make all the cakes in this fashion and coat all sides with bread crumbs. Cover with aluminum foil and refrigerate for 1 to 2 hours before cooking.

Using a very large, nonstick sauté pan or skillet, heat a thin layer of olive oil over high heat. When the oil is hot but not smoking, add a batch of cakes and cook over high heat until golden brown on one side, about 2 to 3 minutes. Carefully turn the cakes and cook on the second side until golden brown. Drain on paper towels and keep the cakes warm while cooking the rest. Serve immediately.

Meat-and-Mushroom Piroshki

Piroshki can also be made with non-yeasted dough, as in this recipe. Beef shin is traditionally used in Russia in the filling of this small, half-moon-shaped pie, but ground beef and sautéed fresh mushrooms make a satisfying and simple filling. The filling is best if made one day ahead. Serve Russian hot-sweet mustard with these savory pies; commercial Russian mustard is readily available in specialty food stores.

Makes 16 piroshki

Filling

1 large onion, cut into small dice

3 garlic cloves, minced

4 tablespoons bacon fat or vegetable oil

¾ pound ground beef

2 teaspoons caraway seed

1 pound medium mushrooms, coarsely chopped

¾ cup minced fresh parsely

¼ cup tomato paste

Salt and pepper to taste

Dough

2 cups unbleached all-purpose flour

½ teaspoon baking powder

¼ teaspoon salt

½ cup (1 stick) unsalted butter, cut into 16 pieces

3 to 4 tablespoons ice water

1 egg, lightly beaten

*P*reheat the oven to 400° F. To make the filling: In a large sauté pan or skillet, cook the onion and garlic in 3 tablespoons of the bacon fat or vegetable oil over high heat for 10 minutes or until golden brown, stirring from time to time. Add the ground beef and caraway seed, and cook over high heat for 3 to 4 minutes, or until the meat just loses its pink color. Remove from heat and place in large bowl.

Heat one half of the remaining bacon fat or vegetable oil in a large sauté pan or skillet. When the fat is hot, add one half of the mushrooms and cook, stirring frequently, over very high heat for 4 to 5 minutes, or until the mushrooms are golden brown and dry. Add to the onion-meat mixture. Cook the remaining mushrooms in the remaining fat over high heat. Add the onion-meat mixture along with the parsley and tomato paste; mix well. Season with salt and pepper and let cool to room temperature before making the pies.

To make the dough: Place the flour, baking powder, and salt in a medium bowl; mix well. Add the butter in small chunks. Using your hands, mix the flour with the shortening, making a coarse, mealy dough. When all the butter has been incorporated into the flour, add the 3 to 4 tablespoons ice water, or just enough to make the dough come together. Turn the dough out onto a lightly floured surface and knead for 2 to 3 minutes, or until the dough is well mixed and smooth. Cover with a damp cloth and let rest at room temperature for 1 to 2 hours. (You may also wrap the dough in plastic and refrigerate it for 1 to 2 days, but be sure to bring the dough to room temperature before working with it.)

On a lightly floured surface, divide the dough into 4 equal balls. Slightly flatten the balls into discs. Divide each disc into 4 equal balls. Cover the balls with a damp cloth and let rest at room temperature for 15 minutes. Roll each ball into a circle about 3 inches in diameter. Place about 2 tablespoons filling on one side of each circle, leaving a ¼- to ½-inch border. Fold the dough over, making a half-moon shape. Press the edges of the dough together to make a tight seal. Begin rolling the edge of the dough by folding the left-hand corner of the dough towards the center of the pie. Continue rolling the edge of the dough so that the edge looks like a twisted rope. Brush the pies with the beaten egg and bake for 25 to 30 minutes, or until golden brown.

Fish-and-Rice Rastegai

Rastegai are traditionally filled with fresh and smoked fish, and are made with a yeasted dough. The characteristic opening in the top of these pies distinguishes these appetizers from other Russian pies such as *piroghi* or *piroshki*. Serve these with sour cream and pickled onions or cabbage.

Makes 24 rastegai

Dough
2 cups unbleached all-purpose flour
1½ tablespoons sugar
½ teaspoon salt

1 package (2 teaspoons) active dry yeast
2 tablespoons warm (105° to 115° F) water
¾ cup warm (105° to 115° F) milk
3 tablespoons unsalted butter, melted and cooled to lukewarm

Filling
1½ large onions, cut into small dice
¼ cup vegetable oil
1 pound chopped boneless white-fleshed fish (sturgeon, snapper, or halibut)
2 cups cooked white rice

¼ cup prepared horseradish
2 teaspoons celery seed
Salt and pepper to taste
½ pound smoked salmon, trout, or sturgeon, sliced into 24 pieces
1 egg, lightly beaten

*T*o make the dough: Place the flour, sugar, and salt in a large bowl; mix well. Add the yeast to the water, stirring to dissolve. Add the dissolved yeast to the warm milk and butter, and mix well. Slowly add to the dry ingredients, stirring with your hand as you go, and forming the mixture into a dough ball. Turn the dough out onto a lightly floured surface and knead for 3 to 4 minutes, or until all the ingredients are combined and the dough is smooth and elastic. Place in a lightly oiled bowl, turn to coat the dough with oil, and cover with a damp cloth or plastic wrap. Place in a warm place (an oven with a pilot light is perfect), for 1½ to 2 hours, or until the dough has doubled in size. Punch the dough down and turn it out onto a lightly floured surface. Divide the dough into 24 equal balls, cover with a damp cloth or plastic wrap, and let rest for 30 to 40 minutes, or until the dough does not spring back when poked with a finger.

On a lightly floured surface, roll each ball out into a circle about 3½ inches in diameter.

To make the filling: In a large sauté pan or skillet, cook the onions in the vegetable oil over moderately high heat for 10 minutes, stirring frequently. Add the fish and cook over moderate heat for 2 to 3 minutes, or until it has just turned opaque. Do not overcook the fish. Remove from the pan and place in a large bowl. Add the rice, horseradish, and celery seed, and mix well. Season with salt and pepper, keeping in mind the smoked fish may be salty. Let cool to room temperature before making the pies.

To assemble: Place several rounds of dough on a flat surface. Place about 1 rounded tablespoon of filling in the center of each round. Place a slice of smoked fish on top of the filling. Fold the dough up around the filling, making a purse-like shape, pressing the two sides of the dough together and leaving a ¾ inch space open in the center of the packet. Place on a lightly greased baking sheet, seam side up, and cover with a damp towel. Let sit in a warm place to rise for 20 minutes. Preheat the oven to 400° F.

Brush the pie with beaten egg and bake for 25 to 30 minutes, or until golden brown. Serve immediately.

Russian Caviar-stuffed Eggs

Hard-cooked eggs stuffed with a myriad of ingredients have been a popular American appetizer for decades, but they are a recent addition to Russian *zakuski*. Stuffed with sour cream and caviar, these rich and colorful eggs are excellent with lemon vodka.

Makes 14 stuffed eggs

8 hard-cooked eggs, halved
½ cup sour cream
½ medium onion, minced

½ teaspoon caraway seed
2 tablespoons minced fresh dill weed, or 1 tablespoon dried
¼ cup lumpfish caviar, rinsed
Salt and pepper to taste

*G*ently remove all the yolks from the eggs and place the yolks in a bowl. Place 14 of the egg halves on a platter, and place the remaining 2 egg halves in the bowl with the yolks. Add the sour cream, onion, caraway seed, and dill weed, and mix well. Add all but 2 tablespoons of the caviar, and gently mix just to incorporate, taking care not to break the grains of caviar. Season with salt and pepper and spoon into the egg halves. Garnish the eggs with the remaining caviar and refrigerate for 1 hour before serving. Serve chilled.

MEDITERRANEAN

The cuisines of the Mediterranean reflect that area's rich and varied history. Over the centuries, countries and cultures borrowed ingredients, cooking styles, and culinary customs from one another, creating a complex patchwork of traditional dishes. As with most classic cuisines, written recipes did not exist until relatively recently. Instead, the custom of passing techniques and knowledge from generation to generation by word of mouth ensured the continuation of these foods.

The custom of serving small plates of appetizers is a popular one in this region. Called *hors d'oeuvre* in France, *mezzes* in Greece, and *tapas* in Spain, tidbits of delectable, often highly spiced foods are almost always served with drinks. This tradition is more commonly seen in taverns, cafes, restaurants, and bars, rather than in private homes, although large family gatherings and holiday feasts are sure to include several plates of pre-meal treats. Appetizers are the most common foods in many of the country-style eating houses throughout the Mediterranean. Wine, aperitifs, beer, sherry, whiskey, ouzo, and flavored spirits are seldom taken alone, and are most always accompanied with a plate of spiced olives, marinated seafood or vegetables, small meat-and-vegetable-filled pies, hunks of cheese, dried fruits, or stuffed grape leaves.

These foods are meant to stimulate the appetite and perhaps calm the effects of too much wine, but often are served in such abundance that the main meal becomes secondary. Drinking, snacking, and talking the hours away is a popular way to spend the afternoon and evening hours. Every large city has its cafe tables of animated young men and women, and in small villages, groups of men, old and young, sit for long periods sipping local wines or spirits, feasting on assorted appetizers, and discussing the world at large. Joyous eating and drinking is not considered a luxury in the Mediterranean, but rather a way of life. When guests come into a home, they are greeted with a beverage and a small plate of fresh vegetables, homemade pickles, olives, local cheese, bread, or perhaps a taste of the dinner to come. Sharing food is an act of love and acceptance, and the spirit of these dishes should be taken as such.

Appetizers from the Mediterranean can be as simple as a plate of luscious red tomatoes warm from the vine, fresh goat cheese, and a few oil-cured olives. More complex dishes such as *briouates* (small meat-, seafood-, or vegetable-stuffed pies), *kibbeh* (meat-stuffed cracked-wheat balls), and *spanakopita* (spinach-and-cheese-filled filo dough triangles) are found not only in upscale restaurants, but in average homes as well. These foods may seem exotic to us, but in their region or country of origin, they are considered standard fare.

Mediterranean cooks are famous for stuffing vegetables with savory fillings of meat, nuts, and other vegetables: spreads made from cooked and ground beans; little pies made with filo dough; and stuffed grape leaves. Olive oil, herbs, spices, assorted cured olives, and vegetables such as artichokes, tomatoes, green beans, eggplant, squash, and lots of onion and garlic form the basis of Mediterranean cuisine. The foods are flavorful, hearty, and loaded with fresh ingredients.

Choose a variety of simple and more elaborate dishes to serve at one time. Many of these recipes hold well at room temperature, making them ideal for parties, picnics, or summer dinners.

Vegetable-Olive–filled Filo Rolls

These delicate filo rolls are filled with a savory combination of Mediterranean ingredients. The roll is baked whole and sliced into rounds after it cools, for easy serving. Three or four slices served with a large green salad makes a good supper. Filling and rolling the tubes may sound time-consuming, but it actually goes quite fast, once you do the first one and get the hang of it.

Makes about 12 rolls

1 large onion, cut into small dice
4 garlic cloves, minced
¼ cup fruity olive oil
1 teaspoon *each* dried oregano, basil, thyme, and red pepper flakes
3 tomatoes, cut into small dice
2 zucchini, cut into small dice
1 yellow bell pepper, stemmed, seeded, and cut into small dice

1 cup cooked artichoke hearts, chopped
¾ cup chopped pitted Kalamata olives
½ cup chopped pitted green olives
Salt and pepper to taste
1 cup (2 sticks) unsalted butter
1 pound filo dough (about 20 sheets)
1¼ cups finely ground almonds

*P*reheat the oven to 350° F. In a large sauté pan or skillet, cook the onion and garlic in the olive oil over moderate heat for 10 minutes. Add the herbs and spices, tomatoes, and zucchini, and cook for 10 to 12 minutes, stirring frequently. Add the yellow pepper and artichoke hearts and cook 3 to 4 minutes. Add the olives and mix well. Season with salt and pepper and let cool to room temperature.

Melt the butter in a small saucepan over low heat. Lay 1 sheet of filo dough, short end towards you, on a flat surface (keep the stack of filo dough covered with a damp cloth or plastic wrap to prevent it from drying out). Brush the filo dough with the melted butter and sprinkle about 2 to 3 tablespoons of ground almonds over the sheet of dough. Cover with a second sheet, and brush it with butter and sprinkle with nuts. Do this with 2 more sheets of dough, brushing with butter and sprinkling with nuts, making a 4-layer stack of dough. Place about 5 rounded tablespoons of filling at the bottom of the stack, across the short end. Roll over the filling once, then fold in the sides of the filo dough (this will prevent the filling from escaping while baking); continue to roll into a tight tube.

Make 4 more rolls, using the same method. Place on a baking sheet and brush with more melted butter. Bake for 35 to 40 minutes, or until the rolls are golden brown. Remove from the oven and let sit for 10 minutes before slicing. Slice into 1-inch rounds and serve immediately.

Mediterranean Filo Rounds

Smoked turkey isn't really a Mediterranean ingredient, but white beans, artichoke hearts, tomatoes, and mint joined with smoky provolone cheese and turkey are an exciting flavor combination. Use marinated artichoke hearts for this dish, and kasseri cheese if you prefer a more assertive cheese flavor.

*Makes 10 to 12 servings (3 to 4 rounds per
    serving)*

1½ cups drained marinated artichoke
    hearts
1 cup drained cooked white beans
¾ pound sliced smoked turkey,
    coarsely chopped
¾ pound provolone cheese, grated
3 tomatoes, cut into medium dice

4 garlic cloves, minced
1 cup chopped fresh mint leaves
1 tablespoon dried thyme
Salt and pepper to taste
1 cup (2 sticks) unsalted butter
1 pound filo dough (1 package or
    about 20 sheets)
1½ cups finely ground almonds or
    pumpkin seeds

*P*reheat the oven to 400° F. Place the artichoke hearts, white beans, turkey, cheese, tomatoes, garlic, mint, and thyme in a large bowl and mix well. Season with salt and pepper; set aside.

Melt the butter in a small saucepan over low heat. Place 1 sheet of filo dough, short end towards you, on a flat surface (keep the large stack of filo dough covered with a damp cloth to prevent the dough from drying out). Brush with butter and sprinkle about 3 tablespoons of ground nuts over the filo dough. Cover with a second sheet of filo dough, brush with butter, and sprinkle with nuts. Continue in the same fashion, using 4 more sheets, making a total of 6 sheets of filo dough. Place about 2 cups of filling at the short end of the filo dough, all brushed with butter and sprinkled with nuts. Roll once over the filling, then tuck in the sides and continue to roll into a firm, tight roll. Place seam side down on a greased baking sheet.

Make 2 more rolls in the same fashion. Place on the baking sheet and brush the rolls with butter. Bake for 30 minutes, or until golden brown. Let sit at room temperature for 20 minutes before serving. Slice into 1½-inch rounds and serve immediately.

Spanakopita

These traditional Greek spinach-and-feta pies make delicate appetizers and are wonderful served piping hot straight from the oven. They also make a good lunch served warm or at room temperature with a Greek salad of tomatoes, cucumbers, Kalamata olives, and marinated onions.

Makes about 40 packets

1 large onion, cut into small dice
3 tablespoons olive oil
3 large bunches fresh spinach leaves, stemmed, washed, and dried
3 eggs, lightly beaten
¾ pound feta cheese, crumbled

3 ounces kasseri or Parmesan cheese, grated
1 tablespoon dill weed
½ teaspoon grated nutmeg
Salt and pepper to taste
1 cup (2 sticks) unsalted butter
1 pound filo dough (1 package or about 20 sheets)

*P*reheat the oven to 375° F. In a very large sauté pan or skillet, cook the onion in the olive oil over moderate heat for 10 minutes, stirring from time to time. Add half of the spinach and cook over high heat until it just wilts but is still bright green. Immediately remove it from the pan and place in a colander. Return the same pan to high heat and cook the second batch of spinach until it just wilts. Drain with the other spinach and place in a large bowl.

Add the eggs, cheese, dill, and nutmeg to the spinach; mix well. Season with salt and pepper and mix well. Refrigerate, covered, for 1 or 2 hours to help the mixture set.

Melt the butter in a small saucepan over low heat. Place 2 sheets of filo dough on a flat surface. Cover the large stack of filo dough with a damp cloth to prevent it from drying out. Cut each sheet of dough lengthwise into 3 long strips. Brush each strip with melted butter and cover with a second strip. Place 1 to 1½ tablespoons of filling at one corner of the short end, fold over, making a triangle shape. Continue folding as you would fold a flag, making a tight, secure triangle. Brush the finished packet with melted butter and place on a lightly greased baking sheet. Make all the packets in this fashion.

Bake for 20 to 25 minutes, or until golden brown. Serve immediately.

Kibbeh
(Meat-and-Onion–stuffed
Cracked Wheat)

This famous dish may seem a bit tedious to make, but once you get the hang of making these terrific stuffed "meatballs," you will find them simple and pleasing to prepare. Use top or bottom round, stew beef, or any inexpensive cut of good-quality beef for this dish.

Makes about 20 pieces

Shells
1½ cups cracked wheat
1 pound beef, coarsely chopped

Stuffing
1 large onion, cut into small dice
3 garlic cloves, minced
3 tablespoons vegetable oil
1 pound beef, minced by hand (not ground)
2 tablespoons ground coriander
1 tablespoon ground turmeric
1½ teaspoons *each* ground allspice and cinnamon

1 medium onion, cut into small dice
Juice of 1 lemon
½ cup ground almonds, pistachios, or pumpkin seeds
Salt and pepper to taste

¼ cup pine nuts
⅓ cup minced fresh mint leaves
2 tablespoons tomato paste
Salt and pepper to taste

2½ quarts vegetable oil for deep-frying
Yogurt-Herb Sauce, following

*T*o make the shells: Soak the cracked wheat in water to cover for 20 minutes. Drain and squeeze out the water, using your hands.

In batches, puree the meat, onion, salt, and pepper in a blender or food processor until smooth. Place the mixture in a medium bowl. Add the soaked cracked wheat and the lemon juice: mix well. Puree the mixture, in batches, until very smooth and doughlike. Place the mixture in a large bowl and add the ground nuts. Beat with a spoon for 2 to 3 minutes. Season with salt and pepper. Cover and refrigerate for at least 1 hour or up to 8 hours.

To make the filling: In a large sauté pan or skillet, cook the onion and garlic in the oil over moderate heat for 10 minutes, stirring from time to time. Add the beef, coriander, and spices and cook over moderate heat for 3 minutes, or until the meat just loses its pink color. Add the pine nuts, mint leaves, and tomato paste and mix well. Season with salt and pepper and let cool to room temperature.

To make the *kibbeh:* Wet your hands and divide the wheat mixture in half. Divide each section into 10 equal pieces, 20 pieces all together. Keeping your hands wet, form each piece of wheat mixture into an oval shape. Using your forefinger, make a hole in the center, gently enlarge the cavity, and make an even-sided shell. Place about 1 to 1½ teaspoons of filling into the cavity and carefully pinch the top together, enclosing the filling and making a tight shell. Make the rest of the *kibbeh* in the same fashion, refrigerating the finished ones as you go.

To deep-fry: Heat the oil in a deep-fryer or in a very large, heavy pot. When the oil is hot but not smoking, add a small batch of the *kibbeh* and cook over moderately high heat until medium brown on all sides, about 3 to 4 minutes. Remove with a slotted spoon or a strainer, drain on paper towels, and place in a warm oven. Repeat to cook all the *kibbeh*. Serve immediately.

To pan-fry: Heat about 2 inches of oil in a large, heavy sauté pan or skillet. When the oil is hot but not smoking, add a batch of *kibbeh* and cook over moderately high heat, turning frequently, until the *kibbeh* are medium brown on all sides. Remove to paper towels, place in a warm oven, and cook the remaining *kibbeh*. Serve immediately.

Yogurt-Herb Sauce

1 cup low-fat yogurt
¼ cup minced fresh cilantro
3 tablespoons minced fresh parsley

Dash cayenne pepper
Salt and pepper to taste

*M*ix the ingredients in a small bowl. Serve at room temperature. Can be stored in a covered container in the refrigerator for up to 2 days.

White Bean–stuffed Tomatoes

You can use unpeeled tomatoes for this rustic dish, my preference, but peeled tomatoes are a bit more elegant. These herbaceous tomatoes are good served with Greek, Italian, or French olives.

Makes 4 to 6 servings

¾ cup dry white beans, washed and sorted
8 cups water
2 bay leaves
1 large onion, thinly sliced
4 garlic cloves, minced
⅔ cup fruity olive oil
½ cup Madeira wine

1 teaspoon *each* dried oregano, thyme, and basil
½ teaspoon dried rosemary
6 to 8 dried black Mission figs, stemmed and thinly sliced
½ pound smoked ham or prosciutto, finely chopped
2 tablespoons sherry vinegar
Salt and pepper to taste
8 medium tomatoes

*S*oak the beans in 4 cups of the water for 8 hours or overnight. Drain and discard the water. Place the beans and bay leaves in a saucepan and add the remaining 4 cups water. Bring to a boil, reduce the heat to moderately low, and cook for 50 to 55 minutes, or until the beans are very tender but not mushy. Drain and place in a large bowl.

Meanwhile, in a large sauté pan or skillet, cook the onion and garlic in ⅓ cup of the olive oil over moderate heat for 10 minutes, stirring frequently. Add the Madeira and cook until it evaporates. Add the herbs and cook for 10 minutes, stirring frequently. Add the figs and ham and mix well. Remove from the heat and add to the beans. Add the vinegar and the remaining ⅓ cup olive oil; mix well. Season with salt and pepper, and cool to room temperature.

Slice about ½ inch off the stem end of each tomato and discard. Using a small spoon, carefully scoop out the pulp of the tomato, taking care not to break or tear the outside shell. Discard the pulp and set the tomatoes upside down on paper towels to drain for 30 minutes. Pat the insides dry with clean towels.

Fill the tomatoes with the stuffing, gently packing the stuffing into the shells and making a rounded shape of filling at the top of each tomato. Serve at room temperature.

Greek Dolmades

Traditional Greek rice-filled grape leaves are much lighter than the lamb-and-rice variety, and just as delicious. These are a little easier to serve if refrigerated for at least 2 hours after they are baked, but they can be served warm on a small plate. Serve with yogurt, grilled lamb kebobs, and tomato-cucumber salad for a full sitdown Greek meal.

Makes 28 to 30 rolls

1 jar (about 35) grape leaves, packed in brine
1¼ cups white short-grain rice
3½ cups chicken stock or broth

1 large onion, cut into small dice
½ cup olive oil
1 tablespoon dried dill weed
½ cup minced fresh parsley
½ cup fresh lemon juice
Salt and pepper to taste

*P*reheat the oven to 350° F. Unfold all the grape leaves and rinse with cool water. Using kitchen scissors, remove the little stem from each leaf and discard. Dry the leaves by wrapping them in layers of paper towels. Set aside until ready to use.

In a small saucepan, bring the rice and the chicken stock or broth to a boil over high heat. Reduce the heat to moderately low, cover, and cook for 25 to 30 minutes, or until the rice is very tender. Place in a large bowl and cool to room temperature.

Meanwhile, cook the onion in 3 tablespoons of the olive oil over moderate heat for 10 minutes, stirring frequently. Add the dill, parsley, and half of the lemon juice, and add this mixture to the rice. Season with salt and pepper, and mix well.

Place 1 leaf, smooth side down and stem end towards you, on a flat surface. Wet your hands and gather about 1 to 2 teaspoons of rice in the palm of your hand, forming a cylinder shape. Place this at the bottom of the leaf. Turn once, fold in the sides of the leaf, and continue rolling, making a firm, tight package.

Place seam side down in a 9-by-12-inch shallow baking pan. Make all the *dolmades* in this fashion.

Drizzle with the remaining lemon juice and oil. Cover with aluminum foil and bake for 20 minutes, or until the *dolmades* are tender and warmed through. Serve warm or chilled.

Egyptian Lamb-and-Currant–stuffed Tomatoes

Savory and sweet, these Middle Eastern stuffed tomatoes are a good choice in summer, when tomatoes are ripe and flavorful. Typically lamb is used in this traditional vegetable dish, but feel free to use beef or pork.

Makes 8 tomatoes

8 large tomatoes
2 large onions, cut into small dice
5 garlic cloves, minced
3 tablespoons olive oil
¾ pound lamb, shoulder or stew meat, finely chopped
1 tablespoon ground cumin

1½ teaspoons ground cinnamon
1 teaspoon ground allspice
2 cups chicken stock or broth
1 cup golden raisins
½ cup toasted pine nuts (see page 8)
¾ cup finely chopped fresh parsley
Juice of 1 lemon
Salt and pepper to taste

*S*lice about ½ inch off the top of each tomato. Using a small spoon, gently scoop out the insides of the tomato, taking care not to break the sides or bottom. Place the tomatoes upside down on paper towels to drain for at least 30 minutes or up to 1 hour. Gently pat the insides dry with paper towels before stuffing.

In a large sauté pan or skillet, cook the onions and garlic in olive oil over moderate heat for 10 minutes, stirring frequently. Add the lamb and spices, and cook over high heat for 5 minutes, stirring all the while. Add the chicken stock or broth and raisins and reduce the heat to moderate, and cook for 30 to 40 minutes, or until the lamb is tender and the liquid has evaporated. Add the pine nuts, parsley, and lemon juice; mix well. Season with salt and pepper, and let cool to room temperature.

Preheat the oven to 400° F. Spoon the filling into the tomatoes and place them in a lightly greased baking pan. Bake for 15 minutes, or until the tomatoes are slightly soft and the filling is warmed through.

Briouates with Assorted Fillings

Kibbeh

Egyptian Lamb-and-Currant-stuffed Tomatoes

Briouates with Assorted Fillings

These Moroccan deep-fried pastries are great for parties because they have three distinctive fillings. I have added some extra spices and flavor to give more dimension to these traditional appetizers. An almost transparent dough called *ouarka* is used in Morocco to make the savory parcels, but commercially made filo dough is just fine. Favorite traditional shapes include triangles, thin tubes, and rectangles, but the instructions here are for triangular packets. Instead of deep-frying the *briouates,* you may brush the tops with melted butter or oil and bake them in a 350° F oven for 20 to 25 minutes.

If you make all three fillings, there will be enough for a 1-pound package of filo dough. If you wish to use only one filling, triple that recipe, or simply make one recipe and have leftover filo dough and fewer packets.

Makes between 32 and 40 packets

Meat Filling

1 medium onion, cut into small dice
2 garlic cloves, minced
3 tablespoons vegetable oil
½ pound lean beef, minced (not ground)
1 tablespoon ground turmeric

½ teaspoon *each* ground cinnamon, cayenne pepper, cloves, and mace
½ cup dried black Mission figs, stemmed and coarsely chopped
2 eggs, lightly beaten
¾ cup minced fresh parsely
¾ cup minced fresh cilantro
Salt and pepper to taste

Chicken Filling

1 large onion, cut into small dice
3 garlic cloves, minced
3 tablespoons vegetable oil
1 tablespoon ground coriander
2 teaspoons *each* cumin seed and ground ginger
1 teaspoon ground cinnamon

1½ cups cooked chicken meat, minced
⅔ cup chopped pitted green olives
2 eggs, lightly beaten
1 cup chopped fresh cilantro
Salt and pepper to taste

Prawn Filling

½ pound small prawns
1 tablespoon unsalted butter
¼ cup all-purpose flour
1½ cups whole milk
1 teaspoon dried dill weed
¼ teaspoon cayenne pepper
Juice of 1 lemon

3 tablespoons capers, drained
Salt and pepper to taste

1 pound filo dough (1 package or about 20 sheets)
2 egg yolks, beaten
2½ quarts vegetable oil for deep-frying

*T*o make the meat filling: In a medium sauté pan or skillet, cook the onion and garlic in the oil over moderate heat for 10 minutes, stirring from time to time. Add the beef, spices, and figs, and cook until the meat just loses its pink color, about 4 or 5 minutes. Add the eggs and cook, stirring constantly, until the eggs set, about 1 minute. Add the parsley and cilantro, mix well, and remove from the heat. Season with salt and pepper. Cool to room temperature before rolling into the filo dough.

To make the chicken filling: In a large sauté pan or skillet, cook the onion and garlic in the oil over moderate heat for 10 minutes, stirring frequently. Add the spices, chicken meat, olives, and eggs, and cook for 2 minutes, or until the eggs set. Add the cilantro and mix well. Remove from the pan and season with salt and pepper. Cool to room temperature before rolling into the filo dough.

To make the prawn filling: Cook the shrimp in boiling water for 2 minutes, or until they just turn pink. Immediately drain and plunge them into cold water. When the shrimp are cool enough to handle, peel them and remove the tails. Chop coarsely and set aside until ready to use.

In a small, heavy saucepan, melt the butter over low heat. Stir in the flour, making a paste. Cook over low heat for 3 to 4 minutes, stirring all the while. Do not let the roux brown or burn. Slowly add the milk in a thin stream, whisking all the while to prevent lumps from forming. When all the milk has been added, bring to a boil over moderately high heat, whisking all the while. Immediately reduce the heat to moderately low and cook for 20 to 25 minutes, stirring frequently, or until the mixture is very thick. Add the dill, cayenne pepper, lemon juice, and capers and mix well. Remove from heat and cool to room temperature.

When the sauce is cool, add the cooked shrimp and season with salt and pepper.

To assemble: Place 2 sheets of filo dough on a flat surface. Cover the remaining stack of filo dough with a damp cloth to prevent it from drying out. Using a very sharp knife, cut the filo dough into quarters. Take 1 to 1½ rounded teaspoons of filling and place at the bottom corner. Fold the filo dough over the filling in a triangle shape, as if you were folding a flag. Continue wrapping the filo dough, making a tight, triangular-shaped packet. Brush the last piece with some egg yolk and complete the packet. Refrigerate until ready to fry. Make all the packets in this fashion, and refrigerate for at least 30 minutes or up to 3 hours before frying.

Heat the oil in a very large, heavy pot. When the oil is hot, gently drop 5 or 6 *briouates* into the oil, and cook until golden brown on all sides, about 1 to 1½ minutes. Remove with a slotted spoon and drain on paper towels. Serve immediately, or reheat in a 350° F oven for 10 minutes.

Kasha Knishes

This classic Jewish-American dish can be filled with either kasha, (a nutty flavored grain milled from buckwheat), seasoned potatoes, mixed vegetables, ground meat, or cheese. Similar to a Russian *piroshki*, the thin dough is wrapped around the filling, making a neat package. It is then baked, and is often served with Russian sweet-hot mustard or sour cream. Chicken fat, or *schmaltz*, perfumes the filling with a rich chicken flavor and adds moisture as well. The amount of fat used in this dish is just enough to make the knishes moist, and flavorful.

Makes 16 knishes

Dough

2 cups unbleached all-purpose flour
1 teaspoon baking powder

Filling

1 egg, lightly beaten
1 cup whole roasted buckwheat groats
  (do not use fine or medium)
1½ cups chicken stock or broth
1 very large onion, cut into small dice
5 tablespoons chicken fat, or 2 tablespoons unsalted butter combined
  with 3 tablespoons olive oil

1 teaspoon salt
¼ cup vegetable oil
2 to 3 tablespoons ice water
2 eggs, lightly beaten

½ cup toasted walnuts, chopped
  (see page 8)
Salt and pepper to taste
3 eggs, lightly beaten

*P*reheat oven to 400° F. To make the dough: Place the flour, baking powder, and salt in a large bowl; mix well. Make a well in the center and add
the oil, ice water, and eggs. Mix with a spoon, incorporating the wet and dry
ingredients to make a smooth dough. Turn out onto a board and knead for 2
minutes. Place the dough in a bowl, cover with a damp towel or plastic wrap, and
let stand at room temperature for 30 minutes. On a lightly floured surface, divide
the dough into 4 equal balls. Slightly flatten each ball to make a disc shape. Divide each disc into 4 equal balls. Cover with a damp towel and let sit at room
temperature for 10 to 15 minutes. Roll out into a circle about 3½ inches in diameter. Cover the dough circles with a damp towel until ready to fill.

To make the filling: In a bowl, combine one fourth of the beaten eggs and the
buckwheat, stirring to coat each grain with the egg. Heat a large nonstick sauté
pan or skillet over high heat. When the pan is hot, add the grain and cook, stirring constantly, over moderate heat for 4 to 5 minutes, or until the buckwheat
turns a shade darker and smells nutty. Add the chicken stock or broth and bring
to a boil. Reduce the heat and cook, covered, over moderate heat for about 20
to 25 minutes, or until all the liquid has evaporated and the grains are tender but
chewy. Remove from the heat and set aside at room temperature to cool.

Meanwhile, in a large sauté pan or skillet, cook the onion in the chicken fat or
butter and oil over high heat for 15 minutes, stirring frequently, or until it is
soft. Add to the kasha, along with the walnuts, and season with salt and pepper.
Add the 3 eggs and mix well.

Place about 1½ to 2 rounded tablespoons of filling in the center of each circle.
Pull the edges up around the filling, completely enclosing it and pinching the
dough to form a tight package. Turn the packages over, place seam side down on
a lightly greased baking sheet, and brush the surface with the remaining beaten
egg. Back for 25 to 30 minutes, or until light golden brown.

Vegetable-Olive-filled
Filo Rolls

Greek Dolmades

Kasha Knishes

LATIN AMERICAN
AND CARIBBEAN

*B*oth Latin American and Caribbean cultures are known for their spicy and satisfying appetizers. Oftentimes, street vendors hawk these hand-held treats, but many are also served in the best restaurants and in private homes. While we can find similar and even identical ingredients used in both Latin American and Caribbean foods, each country or cuisine has a distinct style of cooking and serving food.

In Mexico, appetizers are called *antojitos*. This loosely translates to "desire of the moment", or "little whim" (*ito* is a common diminutive in Mexican Spanish). *Antojitos* are commonly sold on the streets of Mexico, where some of the best Mexican foods are found. Mexicans generally take a small breakfast early in the morning, followed by a large, formal meal in the early afternoon. The remainder of the day is left for snacking, with perhaps a mid-evening meal of coffee and *pan dulce* (sweet rolls).

Street vendors selling *carnitas* (roast pork); tamales made with an assortment of fillings; tacos made with fish, prawns, organ meats, eggs, beef, or pork; enchiladas; flautas; ceviche; *papusas*; *gorditas*; fresh fruit; or *churros*, deep-fried sweet dough dusted with sugar and eaten hot, can be found at any time of day or night. This popular street food is often translated into more formal, elegant appetizers, served on plates before the main course in restaurants and homes.

The cuisines of Mexico are diverse and complex, and depending on what region of Mexico you visit, your meal could consist of anything from goat or pork to fresh prawns and lobster. What many North Americans think of as typical Mexican fare is often tourist food, prepared especially for those with a "different" palate. Mexican food is not traditionally hot or spicy, but piquant salsas and sauces can be added to the finished dish at the table by each diner. Most of the South and Central American and Mexican dishes in this section are classic appetizers that can be found throughout those cultures. *Chiles rellenos* are usually served as an entree, but I think they are light enough to be served as a first course, or as an appetizer to a grand Mexican feast. Chicken-Chili Flautas (page 111), Gorditas (page 110), Corn-and-Cheese Quesadillas (page 115), and Papusas (page 116) are usual Central American or

Mexican fare, but Fried Ham-and Fontina-Tortillas with Red Pepper–Ancho Sauce (page 108) is a dish inspired by Latin American ingredients and created just for this book. Whether you prepare these dishes as a midday snack, as party food, or as an appetizer before a large meal, you will have a rewarding and rich culinary experience.

The foods of the Caribbean are derived from Chinese, Indian, African, Creole, Dutch, French, English, and Spanish influences. When you sample an appetizer from this part of the world you realize how universal Caribbean food really is. Each island has a distinctive style of cooking and serving food, depending on its cultural heritage, but most all Caribbean food is simple, fresh, and pure.

Whether you visit a big city or travel about the countryside, you will see food in every form sold by myriad street vendors. Like the Mexicans, the people of the Caribbean like to snack on savory goodies in the street. Most popular are "stamp and go" (salt cod fritters); boiled or salted peanuts; savory pies made with vegetable, fish, or meat fillings; fresh fruit, tamales; small sandwiches; steamed yams or corn; and grilled meats. Street food aside, small plates of olives, nuts, fish or vegetable salads, elaborate soups, and assorted savory pies are commonly found in the appetizer section of the menus in more formal restaurants. The tradition of warding off the hunger demon with a small snack before the main meal is also observed in most homes.

While there is not an abundance of rolled, wrapped, and stuffed appetizers in the Caribbean repertoire, the few that were chosen for this book are rewarding. Caribbean Sweet Potato Balls (page 103), with their sweet and savory filling; Jamaican Beef Patties (page 105); and Trinidadian Pork Pastelles (page 104) are all rather time-consuming, so plan an afternoon around making these festive and delicious appetizers. I have sampled all three of these dishes while traveling through the islands, and have altered the recipes slightly to make the final product more pleasing. While some of the various steps may be a bit tedious, the recipes are straightforward in preparation and well worth the time it takes to make them. As you roll out the dough for the Jamaican Beef Patties, or stuff the Pastelles, think of warm breezes, hot white sand under your feet, and a crystal clear, aqua-colored ocean.

Caribbean Sweet Potato Balls

Sweet potatoes are one of the favored starches in Caribbean cooking. Green olives and Edam, a Dutch cheese, give these savory appetizers a Continental flavor. The golden brown balls are easy to serve and handle. Prepare the potato mixture a day ahead to allow the flavors to marry.

Makes about 20 balls

2 pounds sweet potatoes or yams, peeled and cut into eighths
1 medium onion, cut into small dice
1 tablespoon ground coriander
1 teaspoon *each* ground cumin, ground allspice, and dried red pepper flakes
Salt and pepper to taste

20 pimento-stuffed green olives
⅓ pound Edam cheese, cut into ¼-inch cubes
2 eggs, lightly beaten
1½ cups finely ground dry bread crumbs
1 quart vegetable oil for deep-frying
Flat-leaf parsley for garnish

Cook the potatoes in salted boiling water to cover for 10 to 15 minutes, or until tender but not mushy. Drain well, place in a large bowl, and mash with a fork. Add the onion, herbs, spices, salt, and pepper and mix well. Refrigerate, covered, for at least 4 hours or for up to 1 day.

Place about 1½ tablespoons of the mixture in your hand. Form the mixture into a ball, and gently press 1 olive and a cube of cheese into the center of the ball. Press the potato mixture around the filling, making a round ball. Make all the potato balls in this fashion, refrigerating them as you go.

Dip the potato balls in the eggs, coating the outside completely. Remove from the eggs and coat with the bread crumbs, once again coating completely. Make all the balls in this fashion.

Heat the oil in a very large heavy kettle or a deep-fryer. When the oil is very hot but not smoking (about 360° F), gently drop a small batch of potatoes into the oil. Cook over moderately high heat for about 2 minutes, or until the balls are golden brown. Remove with a slotted spoon and drain on paper towels. Serve immediately, or keep warm in a 300° F oven until all the balls are cooked. Serve on a large platter and garnish with flat-leaf parsley.

Trinidadian Pork Pastelles

Originally from South America, these pork and cornmeal tamales have been adopted by the island of Trinidad as a favorite snack. A traditional Christmas dish, banana leaf–wrapped *pastelles* are so good they are now eaten all year round. If you cannot find banana leaves in a Latin, Asian or Caribbean market, use corn husks or aluminum foil. A bamboo steamer is ideal for cooking and serving *pastelles*.

Makes about 26 pastelles

Filling

3 tablespoons vegetable oil

1 large onion, cut into small dice

3 garlic cloves, minced

2 jalapeño chilies, stemmed, seeded, and minced

1 pound pork shoulder, minced

1 tablespoon ground coriander

2 teaspoons *each* ground cumin, dried thyme, and dried oregano

1 teaspoon ground allspice

1½ cups chicken stock or broth

3 tomatoes, finely chopped

¼ cup Worcestershire sauce

¼ cup capers, drained

¼ cup black raisins

20 pitted green olives

Salt and pepper to taste

7 to 8 banana leaves, or two 1-pound packages defrosted frozen banana leaves

Dough

¾ cup coarse yellow cornmeal

¾ cup *masa harina*

1½ tablespoons lard or butter

1 teaspoon salt

1½ cups water

To make the filling: In a large sauté pan or skillet, cook the onion, garlic, and chilies in the oil over moderate heat for 10 minutes, stirring frequently. Add the pork, spices, and herbs, and cook over high heat for 2 minutes. Add the chicken stock or broth and bring to a boil. Reduce the heat to moderately low and simmer for 30 minutes, stirring occasionally. Add the tomatoes, Worcestershire sauce, capers, and raisins, and cook over high heat for 10 minutes, stirring frequently, until the tomato has broken down and the mixture is thick and saucy. Season with salt and pepper and let cool to room temperature.

Cut the banana leaves into twenty-six 8-by-10-inch rectangles. Place in a large bowl and cover with boiling water. Drain, refresh in cold water, and pat dry. Stack the leaves and set aside until ready to use.

The cornmeal dough must be warm as you work with it, otherwise it will be difficult to use. For this reason you will need to make 2 batches of dough. The recipe given makes 1 batch. Place cornmeal, *masa harina*, lard or butter, and salt in a large bowl; mix well. Bring water to a boil in a saucepan and add to the cornmeal. Mix well to make a smooth dough. Prepare half of the *pastelles*, then repeat the above process to make the second batch of dough and assemble the remaining *pastelles*.

To assemble the *pastelles*: Place 6 banana leaf rectangles on a flat surface. Using about 2 rounded tablespoons of corn dough for each piece, make 6 balls, and place 1 in the center of each leaf piece. Gently flatten it with your hand to make a circle of dough about 3 inches in diameter. Place about 1 rounded teaspoon of filling in the center of the dough circle and cover with a second circle of dough made with 2 rounded tablespoons of dough. Pat the edges of the dough together, forming a tight seal. Fold one side of the leaf over the filling, fold the second side of the leaf over the first side, and continue wrapping the package with the banana leaf as if you were wrapping a gift. Make all of the *pastelles* in this fashion, and place them on the racks of a large, two-level bamboo steamer.

To cook the *pastelles*: Place a large, two-level steamer over a large pot of boiling water. Steam for 35 to 40 minutes, or until the packages are plump and hot all the way through. Remove the steamer from the water and serve the *pastelles* in the steamer.

Jamaican Beef Patties

These meat pies, originally from the island of Haiti, were first brought to the Islands by the British, but their Caribbean spices and ingredients have made them a popular Jamaican dish. Goat is a common meat in Jamaica, but beef is used in this recipe. When I was in Jamaica, I was served these little meat pies in a round shape, but the half-moon shape is simpler to make and easier to serve and handle.

Makes about 24 patties

Pastry

4 cups unbleached all-purpose flour
1 teaspoon salt
1¼ cups shortening
6 to 8 tablespoons ice water

Filling

1 large onion, cut into small dice
4 garlic cloves, minced
3 jalapeño chilies, seeded, stemmed, and minced
3 tablespoons vegetable oil
¾ pound ground beef
2 teaspoons *each* ground coriander, cumin, and turmeric
1 teaspoon *each* ground allspice and cinnamon

1 green bell pepper, stemmed, seeded, and finely chopped
4 tomatoes, minced
1 bunch green onions, minced
Salt and pepper to taste

2 eggs, lightly beaten

reheat the oven to 400° F. To make the dough: Place the flour and salt in a large bowl: mix well. Cut the shortening into small pieces about the size of walnuts. Add to the flour and, using your fingers, rub the flour and shortening together, making a coarse, mealy dough. Add the ice water and gather the dough into a ball. The dough should be firm and not sticky. If the dough is too dry, add a little more water, but if the dough is too sticky, add just enough flour to make it form a ball. Divide the dough into 2 equal balls and cover with plastic wrap. Refrigerate for at least 2 hours or up to 2 days.

To make the filling: In a large skillet, cook the onion, garlic, and chilies in the oil over moderate heat for 10 minutes, stirring from time to time. Add the beef, herbs, spices, bell pepper, and tomatoes, and cook over high heat for 5 minutes, stirring constantly, until the mixture is thick and saucy. Add the green onions and cook for 1 minute. Season with salt and pepper and cool to room temperature.

To assemble the patties: On a lightly floured surface, divide each ball into 2 equal balls, so that you have 4 equal balls. Flatten into disc shapes, then divide each disc into 6 equal pieces and roll each into a ball. Roll each ball into a 3½-inch-diameter circle. Brush the edges with the beaten egg. Place about 1 tablespoon of filling on one side of each circle, leaving a ¼-inch border. Fold the dough over, making a half-moon shape. Seal the edges with the tines of a fork, and brush with the remaining egg.

Bake on a lightly greased baking sheet for 25 to 30 minutes, or until the patties are golden brown. Remove from the oven and serve immediately.

Peruvian Potato Balls with Pickled Vegetables

The country of Peru has many interesting dishes that showcase the humble potato, a staple of the cuisine. Here is one of my favorites. A sweet-savory stuffing adds a new dimension to these fried potato balls, and the pickled vegetables are the perfect accompaniment. The vegetables are best if made 1 week in advance, but will be perfectly acceptable if made only a few hours before serving.

Makes about 36 balls

5 large baking potatoes, peeled and
   quartered
4 eggs, lightly beaten
3 garlic cloves, minced
1 tablespoon dried oregano
1 small bunch green onions, minced

Salt and pepper to taste
¼ cup raisins
2 hard-cooked eggs, chopped
36 pitted green olives
2 cups finely ground dry bread crumbs
1 cup vegetable oil for cooking
Pickled Vegetables, (following)

ook the potatoes in salted boiling water to cover for 25 to 30 minutes, or until they are tender. Drain and place in a large bowl. Mash with a fork until they are almost smooth. Add half of the beaten eggs, garlic, oregano, green onions, salt, and pepper; mix well. Refrigerate, covered, for at least 3 hours or up to 1 day.

Combine the raisins and hard-cooked eggs in a small bowl. Take about 1½ tablespoons of the potato mixture and form into a ball with your hands. Press a hole in the center of the ball with your finger and fill with some of the raisins and hard-cooked eggs, and 1 olive. Close the potato mixture around the filling, making a smooth ball. Make all of the balls in this fashion and roll them in the bread crumbs, taking care to completely cover the entire surface with the crumbs.

Dip the balls in the remaining eggs, taking care to coat the entire surface with the eggs. Coat with bread crumbs again and refrigerate until ready to cook.

Heat the oil in a heavy skillet over high heat. When the oil is hot, add the potato balls in batches and cook over moderately high heat, turning frequently, until they are golden brown on all sides, about 5 to 7 minutes. Remove with a slotted spoon and drain on paper towels. Place in a warm oven while cooking the remaining balls. Serve immediately with the Pickled Vegetables.

Pickled Vegetables

1 medium onion, cut into ½-inch wedges

1 cup cauliflower flowerettes

1 carrot, peeled, halved, and sliced into ½-inch pieces

⅓ pound green beans, trimmed

6 garlic cloves, thinly sliced

2 teaspoons dried thyme

1½ cups apple cider vinegar

3 cups water

Salt and pepper to taste

lace the vegetables, garlic, thyme, vinegar, and water in a large saucepan. Bring to a boil over high heat and cook for 2 minutes. Remove from the heat, add salt and pepper, transfer to a glass or ceramic bowl, and let cool to room temperature. Store covered in the refrigerator for up to 1 week.

*Peruvian Potato Balls
with Pickled Vegetables*

Red Pepper-Ancho Sauce

*Fried Ham-and-Fontina
Tortillas*

Gorditas

Fried Ham-and-Fontina Tortillas
with Red Pepper–Ancho Sauce

These crispy, smoky flavored rolls take just minutes to assemble and cook. They are excellent for breakfast or brunch, served with scrambled eggs or a mixed-vegetable salad. Use smoked ham or a good-quality baked ham for the stuffing. The smoky taste of the ham complements the sauce, and, since there are only a few ingredients in these tortilla rolls, each flavor should be as clear as possible.

Makes 12 rolls

Twelve 6-inch corn tortillas
¾ pound smoked ham, or 12 thin
   slices

¾ cup chopped fresh cilantro leaves
½ pound Fontina cheese, grated
   (about 2 cups)
2 cups vegetable oil for cooking
Red Pepper–Ancho Sauce, (following)

*P*lace the tortillas on a flat surface. Cover 1 tortilla with a slice of ham. Sprinkle the surface with about 1 tablespoon of cilantro. Place about 2 tightly packed tablespoons of cheese on top of the ham, at the bottom of the tortilla. Roll the tortilla around the cheese, making a tight packet. Make all the rolls in this fashion. To keep the rolls from unwrapping, lay them against each other, seam side down, with a heavy object at one end of the row.

Heat the oil in a large, heavy skillet. When the oil is hot but not smoking, add the tortillas in batches. Cook over moderately high heat, turning the tortillas as one side browns, about 2 or 3 minutes per side. The tortillas should be golden brown and crispy on all sides, and the cheese should be melted. Drain on paper towels and place in a warm oven while cooking the remaining tortillas. Serve immediately on plates with a drizzle of Red Pepper–Ancho Sauce.

Red Pepper–Ancho Sauce

2 or 3 dried ancho or pasilla chilies
3 red bell peppers
2 garlic cloves, chopped

2 tablespoons balsamic vinegar
2 tablespoons reserved soaking liquid
Salt and pepper to taste

*S*oak the dried chilies in water to cover for 2 hours, or until they are soft. Meanwhile, roast, core, seed, and peel the bell peppers (see page 6). Drain the dried chilies, reserving 2 tablespoons of the soaking liquid. Remove the seeds and stems of the chilies and discard.

Place the dried chilies, roasted peppers, garlic, vinegar, and soaking liquid in a blender. Puree until smooth. Season with salt and pepper. Serve at room temperature.

Gorditas

Depending on where you are in Mexico, *gorditas* can be either filled and fried corn tortillas, or small cakes made from *masa harina* and potatoes. I like the latter variety because they are easy to make and serve, and they are delicious, especially with the surprise of spicy chorizo sausage in the center. *Masa harina* is a flour made from ground corn, which can be found in Latin American markets and some major grocery stores. You can substitute very fine yellow cornmeal if *masa harina* is unavailable, but the flavor and texture won't be as authentic.

Makes 30 to 35 patties

4 large baking potatoes, peeled and cut into sixths
2 teaspoons salt
1 tablespoon ground coriander
1 teaspoon *each* ground cumin and dried oregano
2 jalapeno chilies, stemmed and minced

⅓ pound sharp Cheddar cheese, grated
½ cup *masa harina*
½ teaspoon baking powder
⅓ pound chorizo sausage, cut into ½-inch slices
Vegetable oil for cooking
Cilantro sprigs for garnish

Cook the potatoes in salted boiling water to cover until they are very tender, about 30 minutes. Drain and place in a large bowl. Mash with a large spoon to form a fairly smooth mixture. Add the salt, spices, herbs, jalapenos, and cheese and mix well. Add the *masa harina* and baking powder and mix well, using your hands to make a smooth dough. Cover and refrigerate for 2 to 3 hours or overnight.

Place 2 to 2½ tablespoons of dough in the palm of your hand. Form into a ball and push 1 slice of sausage into the center of the dough ball. Enclose the sausage and pat the dough into a round disc shape. Make all the *gorditas* in this fashion. Cover and refrigerate for 1 hour.

In a large sauté pan or skillet, heat a thin layer of oil over moderately high heat. When the oil is hot but not smoking, add the *gorditas* in batches and cook over moderately high heat until golden brown on one side, about 5 to 7 minutes. Using a spatula, carefully flip the *gorditas* and cook on the second side until golden brown. Remove from the pan and drain on paper towels. Serve immediately on a large platter or small individual plates, garnished with sprigs of cilantro.

Chicken-Chili Flautas
with Guacamole

Thicker than traditional Mexican flautas, these crispy-fried flour tortillas are filled with piquant chilies and lean chicken, with a bit of cheese to hold them together.

Makes 12 rolls

Salt and pepper to taste

Guacamole

3 large ripe avocados, peeled and
   seeded
1 or 2 jalapeno chilies, stemmed,
   seeded, and minced
½ small yellow onion, minced
Juice of 2 limes
¼ cup chopped fresh cilantro

4 pasilla or California chilies
3 cups cooked chicken, shredded
½ pound Monterey Jack cheese,
   grated (about 2 cups)
½ teaspoon cumin seed
Ground black pepper to taste
Twelve 6-inch flour tortillas
2 cups vegetable oil for cooking

To make the guacamole: Place the avocados, chilies, onion, lime juice, and cilantro in a bowl. Using a fork, mash the avocado, mixing in the other ingredients as you go. Season with salt and pepper. Place 1 avocado pit in the center of the bowl of guacamole to keep the guacamole from turning brown, or place a piece of plastic wrap directly on the surface of the guacamole. Store at room temperature until ready to use.

Roast, peel, and seed the chilies (see page 6). Cut the chilies into ½-inch squares and combine with the chicken, grated cheese, cumin seed, and black pepper; mix well.

Arrange the tortillas on a flat surface. Place about 2 rounded tablespoons of filling at the bottom of each tortilla. Roll, keeping the filling inside and making a tight roll.

In a large sauté pan or skillet, heat the oil over moderate heat until it is very hot. Add the tortillas in batches, seam side down, and cook over moderately high heat until golden brown on one side. Carefully turn the flautas over and cook the second side until golden brown, about 2 minutes. Remove with a slotted spatula, drain on paper towels, and place in a warm oven while cooking the remaining flautas. Serve immediately with the guacamole.

Chiles Rellenos

I used to think *chiles rellenos* were just for tourists or the unadventurous, but after watching a Mexican cook prepare these stuffed chilies, I decided there was more to this humble dish. If made correctly, the chilies will be tender, the cheese creamy and melted, and the egg batter light and greaseless. A very simple tomato sauce is traditionally served with these stuffed peppers.

Makes 6 rellenos

Tomato Sauce

4 fresh tomatoes, coarsely chopped
2 cups chicken stock or broth
½ cup chopped fresh cilantro
Salt and pepper to taste
6 medium poblano or green California
  chilies

1 pound Monterey Jack cheese, grated
  (about 4 cups)
6 egg whites
5 egg yolks
1 tablespoon flour
1½ teaspoons salt
2 cups vegetable oil for frying

*P*lace the tomatoes and chicken stock or broth in a saucepan and bring to a boil over high heat. Reduce the heat and cook over moderately high heat for 15 minutes, or until the tomatoes have broken down and the mixture is slightly thick. Add the cilantro, season with salt and pepper, and remove from the heat. Set aside until ready to use.

Roast the chilies (see page 6), but be careful not to "over roast" them or they will be thin-skinned and difficult to work with. When the chilies are cool enough to handle, peel, carefully remove the stems and, making a 1-inch incision at the stem end, remove the seeds, taking care not to break or tear the chili. Pat the chilies dry with a paper towel. Pack the chilies with the cheese, and close the openings around the cheese so that it is completely enclosed. Pat the chilies dry again so that the batter will stick.

When you are ready to cook the chilies, place the egg whites in a large bowl and beat until stiff. In a small bowl, combine the egg yolks, flour, and salt and mix well. Fold this mixture into the egg whites until the yolks and whites are just blended. The batter should be light and creamy. Meanwhile, heat the oil in a deep, heavy skillet over high heat.

Dip each chili into the egg batter, completely covering all sides of the chili. Using a spoon, carefully lower the chilies into the hot oil and cook over moderately high heat until golden brown on all sides, about 3 to 4 minutes. When the chilies are completely cooked, remove, using a slotted spoon or spatula, and drain on paper towels for 30 seconds. Serve immediately in a shallow bowl with the tomato sauce.

Corn-and-Cheese Quesadillas

Mexican quesadillas are small turnovers made with either flour or corn tortillas. The fillings vary throughout the different regions of Mexico. Cheese, chilies, chorizo, potatoes, and even brains are traditionally used as quesadilla fillings, and this version draws inspiration from the famous edible corn fungus called *huitlacoche*. This unusual fungus grows on certain types of corn in some areas of Mexico, and is considered a delicacy. Here, sweet corn and creamy white cheese are good substitutes.

Makes 12 quesadillas

3 dried ancho chilies
Kernels cut and scraped from 2 ears
  of white corn

¾ pound Monterey Jack cheese,
  grated (about 2½ cups)
Ten to twelve 6-inch flour tortillas
Vegetable oil for cooking

Soak the chilies in water to cover for 2 to 3 hours, or until they are soft and pliable. Drain and remove the stems and seeds. Cut the chilies into strips and place in a large bowl. Add the corn and cheese to the ancho chilies and mix well.

In a large sauté pan or skillet, heat a thin layer of oil over high heat. Add as many tortillas as will fit. Cook over moderate heat until barely golden brown on the bottom, about 1 minute. Flip the tortillas over and spread about 2 table-spoons of filling on each tortilla, leaving a ½-inch border. Cook over low heat for 1 minute; fold the tortillas over, making a half-moon shape; and cook for 1 more minute, or until the cheese is melted and the tortillas are golden brown.

Remove the tortillas to a warm oven and repeat until all are cooked; serve immediately.

Papusas

These small filled corn tortillas are served in parts of Mexico and most of Central America. They can be filled with shredded pork, cheese, or a combination of both, and are traditionally served with a pickled-cabbage salad called *cortido*. *Papusas* are made with tortilla dough, rather than already cooked tortillas. You can find *masa harina*, the corn flour used to make the dough, in all Latino food stores and some grocery stores. It is easy to work with, and these savory appetizers are simple to prepare.

Makes 12 papusas

Cortido
1 medium onion, thinly sliced
1½ cups shredded green cabbage

1 large carrot, peeled and shredded
3 garlic cloves, minced
¼ cup apple cider vinegar
2 teaspoons dried oregano
Salt and pepper to taste

Filling
4 dried ancho chilies
1 pound boneless pork shoulder
1½ to 2 cups cold water

2 large tomatoes, minced
3 garlic cloves, minced
Salt and pepper to taste

Dough
3 cups *masa harina*
2 teaspoons salt

1½ cups warm water

Vegetable oil for cooking

To make the salad: Combine the salad ingredients in a bowl and mix well. Season with salt and pepper and let sit at room temperature for 30 minutes before serving. Store for up to 5 days in the refrigerator.

To make the filling: Soak the chilies in water to cover for 2 to 3 hours or until they are soft and pliable. Remove the stems and seeds and mince the chilies. Set aside until ready to use.

Cut the pork into 1-inch cubes and place in a heavy pot. Cook over high heat for 2 or 3 minutes, stirring constantly. Add the cold water and bring to a boil. Reduce the heat and cook over moderate heat for 1½ hours, or until the meat is very tender and the water has evaporated. Add the tomatoes and reserved chilies and cook over high heat, stirring frequently, until the meat and tomatoes have broken down, about 5 minutes. Season with salt and pepper and set aside until ready to use.

To make the dough: In a large bowl, combine the *masa harina*, salt, and water, mixing to form a pliable dough. Cover with plastic wrap and refrigerate for 1 hour. Divide the dough into 6 equal balls, then divide each ball into 4 equal balls. Place a piece of plastic wrap on a flat surface. Place a dough ball on top of the plastic and cover with a second sheet of plastic. Roll into a circle about 3 inches in diameter.

To assemble the *papusas*: Remove the plastic wrap from the dough and place about 2 teaspoons of filling in the center of the circle, leaving a ¼-inch border. Cover with a second circle of dough, pressing the filling between the 2 pieces of dough and sealing the edges by pressing them together. Make all the *papusas* in this fashion and refrigerate until ready to cook.

To cook the *papusas*: Heat a very thin layer of oil in a large sauté pan or skillet. When the oil is hot, add the *papusas* in batches and cook over moderate heat for 2 to 3 minutes per side, or until they are golden brown. Drain on paper towels and place in a warm oven while cooking the remaining *papusas*. Serve immediately with the *cortido*.

CROSS CULTURAL

The following recipes do not fit into any specific regional category, therefore they are classified as cross-cultural dishes. While all of the ingredients can be identified as either Italian, Asian, Middle Eastern, Latino, or American, they are combined and prepared in such way that fitting them into specific sections is nearly impossible. I developed these recipes just for this chapter, as they offer a combination of cooking methods, ingredients, and styles that truly makes them international and unusual.

How do we describe food that combines multi-ethnic ingredients in one dish? Take for example Ham-and-Water-Chestnut Fried Wontons (page 126). This dish uses some Chinese ingredients, but the combination of ham and water chestnuts, served with a fresh corn relish, is not traditional Chinese fare. Steamed Cabbage Rolls with Smoked Chicken and Rice (page 129) is another good example of mixing cuisines. Basmati rice, a staple of Indian and Southeast Asian cooking, is combined with Asian spices, sesame oil, and smoked chicken, definitely not a typical Asian ingredient.

I have heard some restaurant chefs describe this type of food as "contemporary urban American cuisine." This rather provocative, if wordy, phrase is based on the idea that large cities, with their international flavor, are the source of a new, exciting cuisine. What once was considered American—meat loaf, mashed potatoes, apple pie, corn, maple syrup, hot dogs—has now joined forces with foods from around the world.

At long last, American cooking is coming into its own, and the rest of the world is paying attention to the work of restaurant chefs throughout the country. The trend towards using fresh ingredients, eating simply, and serving home-style meals has taken hold in many upscale restaurants. Ethnic cuisines are still popular, of course, and probably will be until the end of time. But the United States, the ultimate melting pot, has become so international that it is sometimes difficult to separate "American" food from Italian, Mexican, Central American, Irish, or Southeast Asian foods. And much of what many of us have come to accept as American isn't of American origin at all!

The recipes in this section are colorful, playful, and original. Dishes like these are often created from leftovers, or combine favorite ingredients from several dishes in one recipe. The seafood dishes can be served as elegant appetizers, and the rolled dishes are perfect for cocktail parties. I hope these recipes inspire you to create some New American dishes of your own. Look around—you may have the makings of a cross-cultural dish at your fingertips.

Smoked-Salmon-and-
Potato-filled Sole with
Lemon-Caper Sauce

Shrimp-and-Scallop-filled
Endive with Red Pearls
and Aïoli

Smoked-Salmon-and-Potato–filled Sole with Lemon-Caper Sauce

In this elegant and easy-to-prepare dish, lean fish are rolled with a chive and potato filling and enriched with a luscious tart butter sauce. If you are watching calories, omit the sauce for a low-calorie appetizer.

Makes 15 to 18 rounds

2 large baking potatoes, peeled and
  cut into sixths
¼ cup sour cream
2 tablespoons tomato paste

1 bunch chives, minced
⅓ pound smoked salmon, minced
Salt and pepper to taste
2 pounds boneless fillet of sole or
  other firm white-fleshed fish
2 cups dry white wine

Lemon-Caper Sauce

½ cup dry white wine
½ cup (1 stick) unsalted butter, cut
  into 8 pieces

Juice of 1 lemon
2 tablespoons capers, drained
Salt and pepper to taste

Cook the potatoes in salted boiling water to cover until they are very tender, about 30 to 35 minutes. Drain and place in a bowl. Mash with a fork until fairly smooth. Add the sour cream, tomato paste, chives, smoked salmon, salt, and pepper and mix well; set aside.

Preheat the oven to 400° F. Arrange the slices of sole on a flat surface, long side towards you. With a rolling pin, gently flatten the fillets to an even thickness between ¼ and ½ inch. Place about 4 to 5 tablespoons of filling (depending on the length of the fish) along the length of each fillet. Roll lengthwise, taking care to keep the filling inside. Place the rolls seam side down in a large, lightly greased baking pan. Bake in the preheated oven for 2 minutes, then remove from the oven and add the wine. Bake for 8 to 10 minutes, or until the fish is just opaque. Remove from the oven and let cool to room temperature in the cooking liquid. When the fish is cool, drain and slice it into ½-inch rounds.

To make the sauce: In a small saucepan, bring the wine to a boil over high heat. When the wine is reduced by half, add the butter 1 piece at a time, stirring all the while, until a smooth sauce forms. Add the lemon juice and capers and mix well. Season with salt and pepper and serve in a pool under the fish or drizzled over the top.

Shrimp-and-Scallop–filled Endive with Red Pearls and Aïoli

Rich, decadent, and luscious, this simple appetizer is best served with champagne, but a crisp white wine would also be delicious. Choose your favorite caviar for garnish, but if it is very salty, rinse it in cold water before using or it will overpower the delicate flavors of the seafood. If you cannot find endive, use the small inner leaves of butter lettuce.

Makes about 25 pieces

Aïoli
2 egg yolks
2 garlic cloves, minced
½ cup vegetable oil
¼ cup olive oil
1 tablespoon champagne, white wine,
  or sherry vinegar
Pinch cayenne pepper
Salt and pepper to taste

1 pound medium shrimp
1 pound scallops, cut into ½-inch
  pieces
2 tablespoons olive oil
1 large bunch chives, minced
2 tablespoons minced fresh tarragon
Salt and pepper to taste
25 to 30 large endive leaves
¼ cup red salmon roe or your favorite
  caviar, rinsed

*T*o make the aïoli, place the egg yolks and garlic in a small bowl. Slowly add the vegetable oil in a very thin stream, whisking all the while and making a smooth emulsion. Add the olive oil in a thin stream, whisking all the while. The mixture should be very thick and creamy. Add the vinegar, cayenne, salt, and pepper, and mix well. Refrigerate until ready to use.

Drop the shrimp into boiling water and cook for 30 seconds. Remove from the water and drain well. When cool enough to handle, peel and remove the tails. Coarsely chop the shrimp and place in a bowl.

In a sauté pan or skillet, cook the scallops in the olive oil over high heat for 1 minute, or until they are *just* opaque. Do not overcook the scallops. Let cool to room temperature and add to the shrimp. Add the chives, tarragon, and aïoli and mix well. Season with salt and pepper and refrigerate, covered, for at least 1 hour or up to 6 hours.

Separate 25 to 30 large unblemished endive leaves. Place about 2 teaspoons of filling inside each endive leaf. Garnish with a few grains of caviar and serve immediately.

Chicken-and-Vegetable Mosaic

Once sliced, these precious rounds of chicken and vegetables resemble tiny mosaics. Light and healthy, this finger food makes an excellent spring or summer appetizer.

Makes 30 servings

2 large baking potatoes, peeled and
  cut into sixths
½ cup sour cream
¼ cup tomato paste
3 garlic cloves, minced
1½ tablespoons ground coriander
1 tablespoon ground fennel seed
Salt and pepper to taste
3 large whole chicken breasts with
  skin, boned

1 medium red bell pepper, stemmed,
  seeded, and cut into ¼-inch-wide
  strips
1 large carrot, peeled, cut into ¼-inch-
  wide strips, and blanched
10 to 12 thin asparagus spears,
  blanched
3 tablespoons olive oil
2½ cups chicken stock, chicken broth,
  or water

Cook the potatoes in salted boiling water to cover until they are very tender, about 30 to 35 minutes. Drain, place in a large bowl, and let cool. Meanwhile, preheat the oven to 400° F. When the potatoes are cool, add the sour cream, tomato paste, garlic, coriander, fennel seed, salt, and pepper; mix well, mashing the potatoes as you go. The mixture should be fairly smooth. Set aside until ready to use.

Place the chicken breasts on a flat surface, skin side up. With a rolling pin or meat pounder, carefully flatten, taking care not to rip or tear the skin, to a thickness between ¼ and ½ inch. Turn the breasts over so that the skin is on the bottom and the long side is towards you. Divide the potato mixture among the chicken breasts. Spread the potato mixture over each breast, leaving a ½-inch border. Divide the vegetables among the chicken breasts, arranging them along the bottom to make little bundles. Roll once lengthwise, fold in the ends of the chicken, and continue to roll tightly.

Heat the olive oil in a 9-by-15-inch baking pan in the oven for 5 minutes. Remove from the oven and place the chicken rolls seam side down in the hot oil. Bake for 5 minutes. Remove from the oven and cover with chicken stock, broth, or water and aluminum foil. Reduce the heat to 350° F and bake for 15 minutes. Remove from the oven and remove the rolls from the cooking liquid. If using within the hour, cover and refrigerate the rolls until they are chilled. When the chicken rolls are cold and firm, carefully remove the skin from the outside of the roll and slice the rolls into ½-inch rounds. If you are serving the rolls in several hours or the next day, store the cooled unsliced rolls in the cool cooking liquid until ready to serve.

*Ham-and-Water-
Chestnut Fried Wontons
with Corn Relish*

*Salmon-and-Chive Crepe
Triangles with Two
Caviars*

*Steamed Cabbage Rolls
with Smoked Chicken
and Rice*

Ham-and-Water-Chestnut Fried Wontons with Corn Relish

These slightly spicy, crispy fried wontons are perfect with mixed drinks or cold beer. The colorful fresh corn relish is also good with tortilla chips and crackers. You can make the filling a day ahead, but the wonton skins should be filled just before cooking to prevent the filling from making the wrappers soggy.

Makes about 40 wontons

Filling

½ pound ham steak, minced
1 cup water chestnuts, finely chopped
3 green onions, minced
2 garlic cloves, minced
1 jalapeño chili, stemmed and minced
2 teaspoons ground coriander

½ teaspoon anise seed
1 large egg, lightly beaten

40 wonton skins (about 1 package)
3 tablespoons cornstarch mixed with enough water to make a thin paste (about 2 to 3 teaspoons)
2 cups vegetable oil for cooking
Corn Relish, (following)

Combine all the filling ingredients in a large bowl. Arrange half of the wonton skins on a flat surface. Place about 1 teaspoon of filling in the center of each skin. Brush the edges with the cornstarch wash and cover with a second skin. Make all the wontons in this fashion. Cover and refrigerate for at least 1 hour or up to 4 hours.

Heat the oil in a large heavy pot. When the oil is hot (350° to 375° F), drop 1 wonton into the pot to test the oil. If it sizzles and begins to cook right away, the oil is ready. Cook the wontons in batches of 10 or 12. Do not crowd, or the wontons will not cook properly. Cook until they are golden brown. Remove with a slotted spoon and drain on paper towels. Place in a warm oven while cooking the remaining wontons. Serve with the Corn Relish.

Corn Relish

1 small onion, cut into small dice
½ cup seasoned rice wine vinegar
1½ cups fresh corn kernels (about 2 large ears of corn)
1 garlic clove, minced

1 small red bell pepper, cut into small dice
¼ cup chopped fresh cilantro
1 tablespoon ground coriander
Salt and pepper to taste

Combine the onion and vinegar in a small bowl. Marinate the onion for about 30 minutes. Add all the remaining ingredients and mix well. Serve at room temperature with the fried wontons. This can be prepared up to 1 day in advance.

Salmon-and-Chive Crepe Triangles with Two Caviars

This elegant dish makes a light and pleasant hot-weather appetizer to serve with champagne. You may substitute 1 pound of scallops for 1 pound of the salmon if you would like a mixed fish-and-seafood crepe.

Makes about 40 triangles

Crepes
2 large eggs, lightly beaten
1 cup unbleached all-purpose flour
1 to 1¼ cups milk

5 tablespoons unsalted butter, melted and cooled
½ teaspoon *each* salt, pepper, and fennel seed

Vegetable oil for cooking

Filling
1 large onion, cut into small dice
2 garlic cloves, minced
1 teaspoon ground coriander
3 tablespoons olive oil
1 small bulb fennel, trimmed and cut into small dice
⅓ cup dry white wine

2 cups heavy cream
2 pounds boned salmon, chopped
¾ cup minced fresh chive
Pinch cayenne pepper
Salt and pepper to taste
¼ cup black caviar
¼ cup orange or red caviar

*T*o make the crepes: In a medium bowl, mix the eggs and flour together to form a smooth paste. Slowly add a little milk, making a smooth mixture and stirring all the while with a whisk. Add the remaining milk and stir well. Add the melted butter and seasonings and mix well. Cover and refrigerate for at least 1 hour or for up to 1 day. The mixture should have the consistency of heavy cream. Just before using, thin with a little milk if necessary.

In an 8-inch nonstick sauté pan or skillet, heat a thin layer of oil over moderately high heat. When the oil is hot, add just enough crepe batter to cover the bottom of the pan. Swirl the batter around to all the edges and reduce the heat to moderate. When the edges start to turn golden brown, gently flip the crepe over, using a rubber spatula, and cook the second side until it is a very light golden brown. Remove the crepe from the pan and place on a baking sheet lined with aluminum foil. Make all the crepes in this fashion, using a thin layer of oil each time.

Stack the crepes by slightly overlapping them. Cover with foil, then plastic wrap, and refrigerate until ready to use. You may freeze the crepes at this point for up to 1 month.

To make the filling: In a large sauté pan or skillet, cook the onion, garlic, and coriander in the olive oil over moderate heat for 10 minutes. Add the fennel and white wine and cook for 10 minutes, stirring from time to time, or until the liquid evaporates. Add the cream and bring to a boil over moderate heat, stirring all the while, as the cream tends to boil over. Cook until the cream is reduced to about ¾ cup. Add the salmon and chives and cook for 3 minutes, stirring all the while. Add the cayenne pepper, salt, black pepper, and both caviars, and mix well. Place in a bowl and refrigerate, covered, for at least 6 hours or overnight.

To assemble: Place a crepe on a flat surface. Place about 1 rounded tablespoon of filling on one quarter of the crepe. Fold in half, making a half-moon shape, and fold in half again, making a triangle. Make all the crepes in this fashion and serve slightly chilled.

Steamed Cabbage Rolls with Smoked Chicken and Rice

You may use smoked duck, chicken, or turkey for these spicy cabbage rolls. If steamed and cooled, the rolls will hold together well enough to be eaten by hand. To avoid frustration, buy three heads of cabbage to be sure of having enough large leaves to use as wrappers. It's good to have a few extra, as a torn leaf will not hold the filling and will be very difficult to work with. Use the leftover cabbage for coleslaw or soup. If you do not have a steamer, you can oven-poach the rolls by placing them in a baking pan with ½ cup chicken stock or broth; bake at 350° F for 10 to 12 minutes, or until tender. These light, tender rolls are even better the second day.

Makes about 22 to 25 rolls

3 large heads green cabbage
1 quart water
1 tablespoon salt
1½ cups basmati rice, rinsed
4 tablespoons unsalted butter, cut into
  8 pieces
1 bunch (2 cups) minced green onions
3 garlic cloves, minced
¼ cup sesame oil

1 tablespoon ground coriander
1 teaspoon *each* ground fennel seed
  and dried red pepper flakes
¼ teaspoon ground mace
3 tablespoons soy sauce
1½ cups smoked chicken, duck, or
  turkey meat, minced
½ cup toasted sesame seeds (see page
  8)
2 eggs, lightly beaten
Salt and pepper to taste

ring a very large (10- to 12-cup) pot of water to a boil. Carefully cut out the center core of the cabbages with a paring knife. Carefully lower 1 head of cabbage into the boiling water; cook for 1 minute. Remove with a slotted spoon and drain in a colander. Repeat with the second, then the third cabbage. (Parboiling the cabbage will help you remove the tight outer leaves.) When the cabbages are cool enough to handle, remove the outer leaves, taking care not to tear or break them. Making a triangular shape, cut about ½ to 1 inch of the tough center core from each leaf. This will facilitate rolling the filling inside the leaf, and will make the rolls more pleasant to eat.

In the same pot of water, lower the leaves, 3 or 4 at a time, into the boiling water for about 5 seconds, or until the leaves are very pliable. Immediately remove with a slotted spoon and drain on layers of paper towels. Blanch all the leaves in this manner, draining on paper towels. Dry the leaves by rolling them in layers of paper towels. Set aside until ready to use. (Make sure the leaves are very dry before you begin rolling them.)

Place the quart of water and the salt in a large pot and bring to a boil. When the water is boiling rapidly, add the rice and stir until it returns to a boil. Reduce the heat to moderately high and boil for 12 to 15 minutes, or until the rice is tender but not mushy. Immediately drain and place in a large bowl. Add the remaining ingredients and mix well. Let cool to room temperature.

To assemble: Place 1 leaf, cut side towards you, on a flat surface. If the leaf is still damp, dry it with a clean, dry paper towel or cloth. Place about 1½ tablespoons of filling, depending on the size of the leaf, at the cut end of the leaf, leaving a 1-inch border. Turn once, enclosing the filling. Tuck in the sides of the leaf and continue rolling, making a neat, tight roll. Place seam side down on a baking sheet. Make all the rolls in this fashion.

Steam the cabbage rolls over boiling water for 5 to 7 minutes. Cool to room temperature and serve on a large platter or individual plates.

Smoked Turkey–Three Pepper Rolls with Honey Mustard

Bright crisp vegetables, herbed cream cheese, and smoky meat combine to make these fast and simple appetizers. Feel free to use your favorite commercial mustard, but this sweet-hot version takes only minutes to make and is very good with these rolls. The mustard is best if made 1 week ahead.

Makes about 36 rolls

Honey Mustard

⅓ cup Colman's dry mustard
1 tablespoon white wine vinegar
1 tablespoon cold water
1 tablespoon yellow mustard seeds
3 tablespoons honey
3 tablespoons boiling water
¼ teaspoon salt

¾ pound natural cream cheese, at room temperature
1 tablespoon *each* minced fresh chives, oregano, thyme, and tarragon

Pinch dried red pepper flakes
2 garlic cloves, minced
Salt and black pepper to taste
½ pound mild coppa, sliced very thin
1 pound smoked turkey, sliced ⅛-inch thick
1 large red bell pepper, stemmed, seeded, and cut into julienne
1 large yellow bell pepper, stemmed, seeded, and cut into julienne
1 large green bell pepper, stemmed, seeded, and cut into julienne

To make the mustard: Place the dry mustard, vinegar, and water in a small bowl and stir to make a paste. Add the mustard seeds and honey and mix well. The mustard should be a thick paste. Cover the paste with the boiling water, taking care not to break the surface of the mustard. Let stand for 1 or 2 hours undisturbed. Pour off the water and stir the mustard. Season with salt and pepper. Store refrigerated for several months.

To make the rolls: Combine the cream cheese, herbs, red pepper flakes, and garlic in a bowl; mix well and adjust for salt and pepper. Lay the turkey out on a flat surface and divide the coppa among the slices of turkey. Spread an even layer of cream cheese on top of the coppa. Dividing the peppers equally, place pepper pieces at the bottom of each stack of meats and roll, keeping the meat and peppers tight. Cover and refrigerate for at least 1 hour. Slice the rolls in half and serve on a platter, cut side up. Serve with the mustard.

INDEX

Jalapeño chilies (*continued*)
in Grilled Beef Wraps with Fire Cucumbers and Ice Noodles, 32
in Guacamole, 111
in Ham-and-Water-Chestnut Fried Wontons with Corn Relish, 126
in Hot Chili Dipping Sauce, 27
in Jamaican Beef Patties, 105–106
in Koftas (Indian Meatballs), 75
in Lemon-Chili Dipping Sauce, 37
in Peanut Sauce, 35
in Thai Spinach Packages with Five Jewels and Chili-Honey Sauce, 31
in Trinidadian Pork Pastelles, 104–105
Jamaican Beef Patties, 105–106

Kasha Knishes, 97–99
Kibbeh, 85, 91–92
Chalab, Israeli, 79
Knishes, Kasha, 97–99
Koftas (Indian Meatballs), 75

Lamb
-and-Currant-stuffed Tomatoes, 95
-and-Feta-filled Grape Leaves, 72
in Koftas (Indian Meatballs), 75
-and-Rice-stuffed Zucchini with Yogurt Sauce, Lebanese, 74
Lard, 5
Lebanese Lamb-and-Rice-stuffed Zucchini with Yogurt Sauce, 74
Lemon
-Caper Sauce, Smoked-Salmon-and-Potato-filled Sole with, 122
-Chili Dipping Sauce, Spicy Pork-filled Prawns with, 37

Lentil-and-Pine-Nut-stuffed Eggplant, 73
Lettuce
Leaves, Caponata Wrapped in, 53
Packages, Roast Duck-, with Apricot-Ginger Chutney, 39–40
See also Romaine Leaves

Malaysian Packets, Curried, with Peanut Dipping Sauce, 40–41
Manicotti, Tomato-and-Ricotta-stuffed, with Pesto, 66
Marinade, 32
Masa harina, 12, 104, 110, 116
Meat
-and-Cheese Bread Roll, Three-, 58–59
Filling, Briouates with, 96–97
-and-Mushroom Piroshki, 80–81
-and-Onion-stuffed Cracked Wheat, 91–92
Meatballs, Indian, 75
Mediterranean Filo Rounds, 87
Melon
-Tomato Chutney, Prosciutto-Fontina Rolls with, 61
Wraps, Brandy-Raisin, Smoked Ham and, 65
Menu(s), 17
Asian
mixed, 18
Southeast, 18
Caribbean, 19
cross-cultural, 19–20
Italian, 18
Latin American, 19
Mediterranean, 19
Middle Eastern, 18
mixed ethnic, 20–21
Russian, 19
Mezze, 17, 70
Mezzes, 84